THE HISTORY AND UNCERTAIN
FUTURE OF HANDWRITING

BY THE SAME AUTHOR

A Skeptic's Guide to Writers' Houses

THE HISTORY AND UNCERTAIN FUTURE OF HANDWRITING

Anne Trubek

B L O O M S B U R Y

NEW YORK · LONDON · OXFORD · NEW DELHI · SYDNEY

Bloomsbury USA
An imprint of Bloomsbury Publishing Plc

1385 Broadway	50 Bedford Square
New York	London
NY 10018	WC1B 3DP
USA	UK

www.bloomsbury.com

BLOOMSBURY and the Diana logo are trademarks of Bloomsbury
Publishing Plc

First published 2016

ISBN: HB: 978-1-62040-215-3
         ePub: 978-1-62040-216-0

Library of Congress Cataloging-in-Publication Data is available.

2 4 6 8 10 9 7 5 3 1

Typeset by RefineCatch Limited, Bungay, Suffolk
Printed and bound in the U.S.A. by Berryville Graphics Inc.,
Berryville, Virginia

To find out more about our authors and books visit www.bloomsbury.com.
Here you will find extracts, author interviews, details of forthcoming
events and the option to sign up for our newsletters.

Bloomsbury books may be purchased for business or promotional use. For
information on bulk purchases please contact Macmillan Corporate and
Premium Sales Department at specialmarkets@macmillan.com.

"I never saw a hotter argument on so unexciting
a subject."
—ERASMUS, 1528, "On Handwriting"

CONTENTS

Introduction

HANDWRITING IS HISTORY

ELLIE WAS SITTING at her desk, across from Max and next to Isabel, writing in a small stapled book with a green cover. She had written the title "How the World Works" in large outlined letters and then colored them in using the blue, red, and green markers on her desk. Inside were twelve pages on which she had written in large, neat printed letters.

Ellie (a pseudonym) is a second grader, and I was hanging out in her classroom during the Tuesday morning literacy block of Ms. Hammer's class at an elementary school in Shaker Heights, Ohio. I was there recently to observe a "typical" handwriting lesson in American public schools.

At the beginning of class, I had watched Ellie go to one of the four computers and type in her username to use

Success Maker, a reading program featuring bears that drum when a child gets an answer right. After Ellie finished writing in her book, I squatted next to her and asked her a question: "Which do you prefer, handwriting or typing?"

She thought for several moments, staring at me with a somewhat confused look on her face. Her eyes rolled up towards the ceiling as she contemplated such an odd question, then looked back down at me.

"Writing."

"Why?" I followed up.

"Because when you go to the computer, you have to find a letter and you don't know where it is."

I was surprised by her answer, because at the beginning of the class, all the kids, including Ellie, had raised their hands when asked who wanted to have a turn at the computer. I assumed that, for them, the novelty and ease of keyboarding would be more fun.

When I polled some of Ellie's other classmates, they were equally divided on the question and had a variety of reasons for preferring one method of making letters to another: "Typing is more fun," said one. "Writing is quicker," said another.

A few minutes later Ellie looked back at me. She had changed her mind. "But when you write, your hands hurt, because you have to hold the pencil."

Ellie and the other kids in Ms. Hammer's class, like many

of us, can find pros and cons with the two types of writing instruments in their classroom, pencils and computers. The fact that both handwriting and typing are equal players in Ellie's education speaks to the fact that we are all living through a historic moment in the history of writing: the shift from one technology to another. Ellie and her classmates are at the center of this storm, because they are going to elementary school now, and kindergarten through third grade are the years in which one is typically taught handwriting. Ellie is both lucky and unlucky to be in the middle of this transition. She has two ways of writing at her disposal at a younger age than most Americans have had: she can both type and print. But there is no clear consensus as to what she should be taught. Just printing? Printing and cursive? Or even just "keyboarding"? In a world where you can electronically sign your tax return and where we predominantly use phones for written communication, perhaps Ellie does not need to learn how to use a pencil at all. After all, it makes her hand hurt.

But the prospect of not teaching students handwriting strikes many as unimaginable. The three R's—reading, 'riting and 'rithmetic—have been a core part of American education for as long as any of us can remember. The thought of altering that precept of schooling seems threatening to many, not just because change is often difficult, but because people often carry with them a host of larger associations with handwriting. The ability to write by hand is connected to core values: an educated person must know cursive, some believe. Signing one's name authenticates one as an individual, a unique person. Civilized peoples must teach their children this skill.

These are powerful beliefs, but they are historically and culturally specific. The three R's are themselves an invention of the past century. Many civilized cultures have not developed handwriting. One could consider handwriting as simply one way to make letters, a neutral technology, and conclude that the way we make them is of little import. After all, no one is suggesting we stop teaching the expression of ideas through written language. This shift from handwriting to keyboarding could be seen as innocuous as, say, teaching high schoolers how to drive only cars with automatic transmissions.

However, since handwriting is bound up with connotations that propel it beyond being simply a fine motor skill, the prospect of its disappearance is threatening and anxiety producing. The current shift from one writing technology to another is as jarring and culturally significant as when the printing press was invented. In the sixteenth century, monks decried the horrors of printed books, which they were sure would be full of mistakes. Today we find ourselves unsure of handwriting's future, and it has become the focus of a very similar anxiety. Will people who text a lot become less literate? Does Twitter spell the end of complex, lengthy writing?

These anxieties and worries aren't new to the twenty-first century, and if history is any guide, new technologies do not kill off previous ones. Writing did not kill speech, but speaking took on new valences as writing came to compete with it; indeed, the ancient Greeks argued orality was a more complex form of communication than writing. We see this happening now, as handwriting is lauded as something that embodies positive personal qualities: rigor over facile information processing, individual emotion over impersonal mechanization.

Writing of any kind—be it on computer, on a typewriter, on papyrus, or in stone—is not natural. It is artificial, a man-made technology. Speech will always be more "personal" and "natural" than any type of writing.* But technologies have much to recommend them. We will lose something as we print and write in cursive less and less, but loss is inevitable. In fact, it may be the only constant in the history of handwriting. I regret how little is now written in clay or stone, with its distinct heft; I miss the physicality of typewriting, the hard shove of the carriage return and the satisfying flick of the completed page out of the platen. Yet I am thrilled I can write this book on a computer, which makes deleting poorly written

---

* Voice recognition software may be the "purest" writing technology ever invented, as it returns us to the realm of speaking, something most humans learn autonomously, whereas writing must be taught.

paragraphs easy and allows me to change and refine my ideas as I compose.

So should Ellie learn cursive? Probably not. It will only really prepare Ellie for third grade, not life. But the history of handwriting is replete with lessons once taught to generations now forgotten—and some that resonate with us anew. Children have been learning to write for some six thousand years. In those early classrooms, teachers taught how to press wedge-shaped marks into wet clay. As unfamiliar a way to learn one's letters as that might sound, the tablets they produced have much in common with how many of us—including second graders—write today.

Chapter 1

THE STRANGELY FAMILIAR VERY FAR PAST

CUNEIFORM, HUMANITY'S FIRST writing system, was invented some five thousand years ago in what is now southern Iraq, and it was most often written on clay tablets a few inches square and an inch thick. Hundreds of thousands of tablets have been discovered by archaeologists over the centuries, and they are held by many museums and libraries around the world, including the Morgan Library & Museum in New York. When I visited the Morgan to view cuneiform, Sidney Babcock, curator and department head, Ancient Near Eastern Seals & Tablets, invited me to pick one up. "Really? I can touch it?" I asked. "Absolutely," he responded. "The oil on your hands won't hurt them. And they won't break—they've lasted this long!"

To be so close to these tablets, which are mind-bogglingly old, was stunning. Vellum, parchment, papyrus, and paper—other writing surfaces people have used in the past—deteriorate easily. But not clay, which has proven to be the most durable, and perhaps most sustainable, writing surface humanity has ever employed.

Gingerly, I brought the tablet close to my eyes. The clay was cool to the touch. Palm-sized and pale brown, it was full of tiny incisions. Although I had seen images of cuneiform before my visit to the Morgan, I underestimated how much the reproductions had been magnified. I imagined the tablets would be the size of my iPhone, but most were half that. And the marks were tiny. Babcock used this analogy to describe the size of the writing: "Find the second portrait of Lincoln on the penny. You know, the one of his statue inside the Lincoln Memorial on the obverse? That's how small the script can be."

The tablet, cool and fitting nicely in my palm, felt somehow comforting. There was something indescribably affective about touching it, and something familiar, too—not unlike holding my smartphone, upon which I often make marks.

"Cuneiform," which means wedge-shaped, is a term the Greeks used for the look of the incisions. It was used to write at least a dozen languages, just as the alphabet that you are reading is also used for many other languages. It looks like a series of lines and triangles, as each sign comprises marks—triangular, vertical, diagonal, and horizontal—impressed onto wet clay with a stylus, a long, thin instrument similar to a pen. Clay tablets were so central to cuneiform they became part of one Sumerian word for "writer," *dubsar*, which combined the word for "tablet," *dub*, with *sar*, from the verb for "writing," which means to go fast and straight. A *dubsar* was a writer or scribe who could write quickly and in a straight line on a tablet. Sumerians also integrated an old technology into another verb used for "writing," *hur*, which also means to draw or trace. What was to them a new technology, writing, was associated—linguistically, at least—to an older one, drawing, which they had previously done on pottery.*

Deciding to use clay for a writing surface was ingenious. As a result, many more examples of Sumerian writing have survived than more recent writing done by ancient Greeks, Romans, medieval Europeans, and even, proportionately, writing done after the invention of the printing press. If the Greeks had written on clay, the Library of Alexandria would have survived the flames. (Egyptian papyrus, the second oldest writing surface, has also lasted better than many forms that came after it because of the Egyptians' practice of burying documents in sealed containers.) We have a glut of cuneiform but a

---

* We do this kind of linguistic repurposing today all the time. For instance, we talk about "browsing" the Web. The word "browse" was originally used to describe a different action: something one did in bookstores and antique shops.

paucity of cuneiform readers—only a few hundred in the world—so only a fraction of the discovered tablets have been translated. Still, they have not been lost to posterity, even if they have been ignored. Each time a cuneiform-using city was burned down during the past five thousand years, the clay hardened and became even more indestructible.

Of course, cuneiform wasn't the first method by which human beings made marks. Cave paintings, tally sticks, and memory boards all predate cuneiform. But those are forms of information storage, and thus considered by most linguists to be proto-writing. Most agree that cuneiform did begin as proto-writing—like African drumming and Incan *quipu*s, record keeping by means of knotted cords— and evolved into the first full-fledged writing system, with signs corresponding to speech.[1] The roots of cuneiform lie in tokens, or chits, used by Sumerians to convey information. They would take a stone and declare it a representation for something else, perhaps a sheep. A bunch of stones might mean a bunch of sheep. These stone tokens would sometimes be placed in a container and given to someone else as a form of receipt—not that different from what we do today when we hand over pieces of paper with numbers on them to buy a quart of milk, and the clerk gives us back another piece of paper with numbers on it to confirm the transaction.

By 3000 B.C.E. the Sumerians had taken this system to another level of abstraction and efficiency, moving it from proto-writing to writing. They began using clay envelopes instead of cloth envelopes, and instead of putting stones inside of them, they stamped the outside of the envelopes to indicate the number and type of tokens being conveyed.

Gradually, Sumerians developed symbols for words. At first these phonemes symbolized concrete things: an image of a sheep meant a literal sheep. Then another leap of abstraction was introduced when symbols were developed for intangible ideas, such as God, or women. Cuneiform, in other words, evolved from a way to track and store information into a way to explain the world symbolically. The marks became more abstract over time as well, evolving into signs that look nothing like what they refer to, just as the letters *s-h-e-e-p* have no visual connection to a woolly four-legged animal. These marks and signs took the form of triangular wedge shapes.

Cuneiform marks became more abstract because they made the system more efficient at a time the Sumerians' society was becoming more complex. The origins of writing lie in their need to keep better records—not, as many might assume or wish, to express oneself, create art, or pray. Most agree cuneiform developed primarily for accounting purposes: While we can't know about tablets that have been lost, the majority of those that have been excavated and translated contain administrative information.

Mundane as this story is concerning why writing was invented—to record such things as sheep sales—the story of how cuneiform was later decoded is spectacular. For hundreds of years no one could read it. Even though cuneiform was used for millennia—and much of it, incised on rocks in Persia, was in plain view for centuries after it ceased to be used—the language was unintelligible for almost two thousand years. Not until 1837, after British army officer Sir Henry Rawlinson copied down inscriptions from the steep cliffs of Behistun, in western Persia (now Iran), could anyone know what the marks said.

How those marks were made continues to defy logic or explanation: The angle and height of the incisions seem to preclude the possibility of a chiseler on a ladder. Rawlinson at least figured out how to copy the marks by making paper impressions as he stood, perilously, on the ledge. Then he took them home and studied them for years to determine what each line stood for, what each group of symbols meant. Eventually he decoded the markers that had sat in the open for some five thousand years, thereby cracking the cuneiform code. (The inscriptions describe the life of Darius the Great, king of the Persian Empire in the fifth century B.C.E., as well as his victories over rebels during his reign.) Similar to the Rosetta stone, on which the same text is written in hieroglyphics, demotic, and Greek, the cliffs of Behistun contained the same words written three times in three different languages: Old Persian, Elamite, and Babylonian. None of these languages were known, but several scholars, over time, slowly cracked the code by first discovering the key to reading Old Persian and then, because the same words were written in each language, decoding the other two inscriptions.

Once the language could be translated, scholars learned about Sumer, including how Sumerians taught cuneiform to their children. We now know quite a bit about what Sumerian children did in a penmanship class. Their activities were remarkably similar to what happens in Ms. Hammer's second-grade class today.

Having invented the first writing system, Sumerians also established the first schools to teach writing. Schooling was entirely devoted to teaching writing. (The Sumerian word for "school" is *edubba*, or tablet house.) But schooling was far from universal. Only a tiny percentage of Sumerians were taught to write—primarily the sons and, occasionally, daughters of the most privileged in Sumerian society.

A wellborn boy started school at around age seven. During class he would sit, probably outside, on the ground, and his first lessons would be about tablet making: He had to make his own writing surface, too. (Today, of course, children are not required to make their own paper.) His teacher would give him a piece of wet clay and tell him to mold it into one of several shapes and sizes, each of which indicated a different purpose for the tablet: Some were round, some square, some large, some tiny. Round tablets were used only for school assignments. The most common shape was a palm-sized rectangle.

To write on his tablet, the boy used a stylus usually made from a reed, since cuneiform requires no ink or graphite; one cuneiform scholar terms it "writing with shadows." Then, with his tablet and stylus in hand, he was taught how to score the tablet into columns and lines that would guide the marks. The columns not only helped the boy keep his words straight but also divided the communication into manageable units, like a page or a paragraph is used by us today. After scoring his tablet, he would then make signs, pressing his stylus into the clay in the proper direction and at the proper depth.

Stylus technique was complicated. The tip of the stylus was triangular, and turning it caused different slants and directions for the marks—some went deeper than others, some went horizontally or vertically, and the bottom of the stylus would make a round mark—each with a distinct meaning. Writing was two-handed: Cuneiform writers held the stylus in one hand and the tablet in the other, turning both as they went, an action requiring practice and training to master.

Students were taught the symbols for words using principles of linguistics and phonics that are still valued as pedagogical principles.* There were no textbooks or lesson plans; instead, teachers memorized assignments—perhaps from their own schooldays—and taught their students to do the same. No one composed writing; all the students did was copy, following drills to improve memory and fine motor skills. In one exercise, teachers would help students learn their marks by writing words on one side of a tablet and then give the tablet to the student, who would turn it over and use the other side to try writing the same words—not unlike a blackboard demonstration.

Years of study were needed to become a scribe. That the training was so extensive makes sense, given how small the script and tablets are and the complexity of the marks themselves. Also, cuneiform became more complex as it evolved, and new signs were added. Students had to memorize hundreds of signs, and some would continue, after learning the basics, to advanced studies. They could specialize in copying legal documents or in temple administration. The most advanced students were allowed to copy hymns and epics.

---

* As Maryanne Wolf argues in *Proust and the Squid: The Story and Science of the Reading Brain* (New York: Harper, 2007), the pedagogy Sumerians used to teach their children—by emphasizing categories of words, such as types of trees, animals, stones, plants, clothing, and food, as well as the practice of copying—is similar to contemporary educational practices.

Remarkably, all cuneiform marks look identical across tablets. Some scribes left small marks, called colophons, on their tablets, attesting to the authenticity of what had been written and honoring Nabu, the god of scribes, but the colophon was written in a script indistinguishable from the other words on the tablet. The fact that, of the thousands of tablets found—many from the same archaeological site—none are written with an identifiable hand becomes even more astonishing in light of the complexity and intricacy of cuneiform.

The first handwriting, then, was not the least bit personal. Based on their output, scribes were more like human computer keys than they were individuals expressing ideas. However, Sumerians did have a way to distinguish themselves: Each one had a unique seal.

All Sumerians, even the illiterate, carried seals: small, cylindrical pieces of stone (not clay) upon which were carved, intaglio-style, raised words and images. Seals had holes through them and every Sumerian hung his or her seal around the neck. And, just like fingerprints, no two seals were the same.

Cuneiform seals were the Sumerian version of signing one's name in ink. To witness a marriage, a Sumerian would roll her seal over a wet tablet, making a base impression on the clay shallower than the marks contained within it, similar to a rubber stamp. Seals were so central to Sumerian society that experts have identified "canceled" seals—the equivalent of cutting up a credit card—as well as forged seals and seals with lines scratched across them, perhaps made after someone died.

Although each seal was made from stone, Sumer had no stones: It was a flooded desert plain. Every seal, therefore, had to be imported. Some of the stones have been identified as coming from as far away as modern-day Afghanistan and Egypt, but how or why they were transported is unknown.

To us, one's signature is tied ineluctably to his sense of self. Signatures are not reproducible: There are laws against forging them. But for Sumerians the opposite was true: seals were their signatures, and they were reproducible. Each time a Sumerian rolled her seal across clay, it looked exactly like the last time she did it: Again, the seal functioned much the same way as a rubber stamp does today. Seals were a form of identity akin to credit cards: both reproducible (you used them to make the same mark over and over) and unique (they identified one unique individual).

Cuneiform, as a writing system, is dead in the sense that Latin is dead: No one writes or converses in it. But it is not gone. One can buy *Complete Babylonian: A Teach Yourself Guide* by Martin Worthington and, indeed, argue persuasively that cuneiform was the most influential writing system in human history: Fifteen other languages developed from it, including Old Persian, Akkadian, and Elamite. Sumerian was taught as a classical language for generations after it ceased to be a living language. It was taught to those who spoke Aramaic and Assyrian but who read, copied, and recopied Sumerian literary works. By 1600 B.C.E. no Sumerian speakers were alive, but Sumerian was still used for another thousand years. When one form of writing "dies," it takes an inordinately long time to go extinct, if it ever does.

Eventually, Aramaic and Akkadian replaced Sumerian. Writers stopped using clay in favor of papyrus. And a new word, "scribe," replaced the Sumerian word, "tablet writer." The transition was slow, with several systems being used simultaneously; clay continued to be used even after most people had shifted to papyrus.

Indeed, this transition is familiar: The simultaneous use of different writing technologies was happening in the coffee shop where I typed this chapter. Looking up, I saw people using a pen to annotate a paperback, a cell phone to text, a laptop to write, and a pencil to take note of a transaction at the cash register. Some days, a twentysomething hipster comes in with his manual Remington typewriter, too.

We may, in fact, be becoming more like the Sumerians with every passing year. Most of us carry around small, palm-sized writing tablets made of a durable material. And cuneiform feels—materially—more similar to my daily experience of writing than do the sheets of paper in elementary school classrooms.

Chapter 2

THE PROBLEM WITH VERY
BEAUTIFUL WRITING

L IKE THE SUMERIANS, the ancient Egyptians sent children to school exclusively to learn how to write. But Egypt restricted literacy much more than Sumer did. Only boys from the most elite families were taught writing, and thus only a tiny fraction of the population was literate. Most walked through temples and along walls of buildings carved with hieroglyphs they were unable to decipher.

For most of writing's history, access to literacy has been extremely restricted; and while literacy rates fluctuate throughout epochs, in Egypt it was perhaps the lowest of any civilization. The beauty of hieroglyphics is, in fact, related to their exclusivity. When a culture's writing is a rare, exalted, and magical thing, it is also often elitist.

Chinese, Arabic, Hebrew, and other scripts share a correlation between beautiful handwriting and the sacred, but none are as elaborate and restricted as hieroglyphics were during their long reign.

The first and longest-used Egyptian script, hieroglyphics, was in use for three and a half millennia, much longer than the Roman alphabet has survived thus far. Cuneiform and hieroglyphics are often discussed together as the earliest scripts (hieroglyphs are thought to have been influenced by cuneiform, and invented shortly thereafter, although there is no hard evidence to confirm that or to precisely date either's first appearance), but they are vastly different from each other in almost every respect. Cuneiform was adopted by many different peoples and cultures, while hieroglyphs had little influence on other languages and scripts. Part of the reason for this insularity lies, again, in beauty: Hieroglyphs were as much an art form as they were a means of information storage. These scripts are as much something we look at for their visual beauty as they are something we look through for their information.*

Unlike cuneiform, we know little about how hieroglyphs,

---

* Tellingly, many books on the origins of these scripts are classified in American libraries as art, not history.

a largely logographic and pictographic system, arose.* For centuries there were six hundred to seven hundred hieroglyphs, carved onto temples, tombs, and jewelry as well as written on papyrus. Then, during the Ptolemaic period in the fourth century B.C.E., there were suddenly six thousand to seven thousand in use. As the writing system became developed and institutionalized, it became more elaborate, making it even more difficult for novices to decipher and master and therefore further blocking access to literacy.†

Elite Egyptian boys were tasked with a difficult skill to master. Their medium was papyrus, a writing surface made from the marshy plant of the same name. Papyrus grew along the river, some plants as tall as ten feet. (In ancient times it grew in abundance; by the eighteenth century, it would be extinct.) It was an extraordinarily clever choice for a writing surface: flexible, durable, inexpensive, and reusable. It was made by taking off the rind, beneath which were soft insides that were cut into

---

* Egypt straddles two traditions in the history of writing: Since hieroglyphics (unlike cuneiform) were important for the development of the alphabet, it is important to understanding much of subsequent Western culture described in this book; but in its insularity it is more similar to other, non-Western scripts not discussed here.

† In fact, one might wonder whether the creative blossoming of text messaging today might be creating a similar phenomenon, at least for adults who struggle to decode the never-ending invention of acronyms and emojis that teenagers frequently use to communicate.

strips. These were wetted and then pounded together until they stuck to each other, the process repeated until a twenty-foot scroll was formed that would, after it was written on, be rolled up, tied with a string, and marked with a unique clay seal indicating the scroll's owner. Like the Sumerians, the Egyptians carried seals, sometimes on one of their fingers, the origin of the term "ring finger."[1]

With a blank roll of papyrus on his left, a student would pull a scroll until one section sat comfortably across his lap; this constituted a "page" of hieroglyphs. On his lap rested a scribal kit, an exalted, sometimes religious object; one was placed in King Tut's tomb that contained two inkwells, one red, one black, and a vessel for water used to wet the ink. The black ink was made from carbon, the red ink from an iron oxide. The boy used the red ink—as would the Christians centuries later (think "red-letter day")—only for important words and headings. His ink choice also had religious resonances; he would switch from black to red, a color associated with danger, to write the word "evil," for example.

To write—or, perhaps more precisely, to paint—the boy took up a long, thin hollowed-out tool made out of the reeds that grew in the fields around him. He chewed on one end of the reed to make it into a brush. Dipping his brush in the ink, he copied homilies, such as:

Be a scribe, so that your limbs may become sleek, that your hands may become soft, that you may go forth, admired, in white attire and that your courtiers may salute you.

or one found on a scrap of papyrus now in the British Museum:

Apply yourself to writing zealously; do not stay your hand . . . pleasant and wealth abounding is your palette and your roll of papyrus.[2]

He wrote from left to right until he ran out of space on the papyrus that covered his lap. When the papyrus wrinkled, he used a stone to smooth it out.

The boy's school was associated with one of the town's temples. Before he was allowed to write on papyrus, he had to practice making hieroglyphs on clay shards called ostraca and on boards covered with gesso, a plaster mixture that created a surface somewhat like a chalkboard. Only when he proved himself capable was he allowed to use papyrus to create the images that served as symbols for speech: the ducks and crocodiles and men that we think of when we imagine Egyptian hieroglyphics, which were as much decorative as they were communicative.

While children like Ellie spend about three years learning twenty-six characters, as well as reading, math, and other subjects, the rare child in ancient Egypt who was allowed to write spent at least five years learning how to do so. Indeed, hieroglyphs are perhaps the most difficult and elaborate writing system the world has ever created.* The education necessary to master hieroglyphs was similar to but even more intense than that which is necessary to learn classical Chinese or Japanese today. And, like those languages, Egyptian stood then, as it stands now, as a language in and of itself, resistant to change and adoption by other peoples. Nonetheless it was long-lived: Hieroglyphic inscriptions have been found dating as late as 394 C.E., thousands of years after the system was invented.

Unlike cuneiform, much of what remains of Egyptian hieroglyphics today is religious, not economic. Hieroglyphs were used for formal purposes: writing on diplomas and wedding invitations, for example. It was also used for legal papers and bureaucratic memos, so much so that scholars who initially believed Egyptians to be a philosophical culture changed their minds when they realized how thoroughly bureaucratic so many of the documents were.[3] But most of the writing remaining in hieroglyphics glorifies

---

* As Wolf writes in *Proust and the Squid*, "By the first millennium B.C.E., the brain of an Egyptian scribe may well have required far more cortical activation and cognitive resources to handle the encrypted meanings than was required for most other writing systems in all of history."

the pharaoh and the gods. Whether or not this means religion played a larger role in Egypt than in Sumer, where
economic motives stimulated cuneiform, remains uncertain.
Egyptians used the fragile papyrus as their writing surface,
so less of it remains than sturdier Sumerian clay. Likewise,
Egyptians may also simply have worked harder to preserve
the religious texts than they did the bureaucratic ones.[*]

Also, hieroglyphs were only one of several scripts the
Egyptians used. For the bureaucratic communication they
were so fond of, like temple business or records of goods
and services, the Egyptians gradually shifted to an easier,
more pragmatic script: hieratic, perhaps the first true
"handwriting" in our history—a less formal and ritualized
script than hieroglyphics. Eventually, hieratic script came
to be used religiously as well; for example, the Book of the
Dead is written in hieratic. Then, as the centuries
progressed, hieratic became identified with religious
writing; hence the word "hieratic" itself, which was coined
by the Greeks and means priestly.

The third Egyptian script the Greeks called "demotic,"
or popular, which, despite its name, was still reserved for
the ultra-elite. The Egyptian word for this script is more
apt, translating as "writing of documents." Demotic was

---

[*] Of course, there are an enormous number of remaining hieroglyphics that were chiseled on walls, tombs, and buildings.

in effect the first cursive script. It could be written quickly and was originally used, like hieratic, for administrative purposes. Then, as the centuries passed, it, too, took on a religious and literary role.

If Sumerian scribes were functionaries preserving culture and helping business get done, in Egypt they were part of the priestly and ruling class. So revered were scribes that commemorative statues showing scribes sitting, legs crossed, their writing boards and palettes across their laps, were commissioned by Egyptian princes and high officials who were not scribes themselves but wanted a piece of the status a scribe held. Scribes even had tax-exempt status. The Egyptian word for "writing" translates as "words of the gods." The god of the scribes was Thoth, one of the most important of the gods. Thus, given this tinge of importance, writing and writers were equally touched with prestige and the sacred. One Egyptian saying about scribes extolled: "You are one who sits grandly in your house; your servants answer speedily; beer is poured copiously; all who see you rejoice in good cheer. Happy is the heart of him who writes; he is young each day." Another observed: "Yes, for the scribe, whatever his place at the residence [the pharaoh's court], he cannot be poor in it."[4]

What scribes wrote, however, was tightly controlled, and only what the pharaoh wanted written. Egyptian scribes were the conservative protectors of the status quo. The few who knew how to write were also the few who ran the temples, armies, and government. As scholar Barry Powell writes, "When we study 'the Egyptians,' really we study the thought, religion, achievements, and aspirations of this tiny elite. About the thoughts of those who worked the fields from birth to death, then were buried in unmarked graves at the edge of the desert or thrown into the Nile, we have no information. Writing preserves only the thought of literate peoples."[5] The brushstrokes made on papyrus were as inscrutable and illegible to the overwhelming majority of Egyptians as they are to most of us today. And of those majority we have no written record.

Hieroglyphics eventually died out. But civilization, of course, did not. The ancient Greeks, who famously believed in education for more than just the elite, invented an easier—the easiest ever—writing system: the first true alphabet. One might assume, then, that the next chapter in the history of handwriting would be one of increased literacy. But, in fact, writing took a big step backward.

Chapter 3

THE LONG TAIL OF GREECE
AND ROME

M OST OF US take it as a truism that writing is good, ennobling, and central to being an educated citizen. Socrates, ancient Greece's greatest thinker, believed the opposite. He argued vehemently, through speeches Plato later wrote down, that writing caused humans to become less intelligent, less civilized, and less creative. As he put it: "A reader must be singularly simple-minded to believe that written words can do anything more than remind one of what one already knows."[1] For Socrates, mastering orality, not writing, was the epitome of knowledge. Having a robust, complex oral mind would ensure history would be preserved: "If men learn [writing], it will implant forgetfulness in their souls; they will cease to exercise memory because they will rely on that which is written."[2]

Socrates also worried writing would stunt complex thoughts. We can only internalize concepts, he said, if we memorize them, and we can only fully develop those concepts if we talk them out. For Socrates and many other Greeks, speech was the most rarified, complex form of knowledge and expression.

Writing does decrease the human capacity to remember, to mentally retain and file facts, ideas, and experiences for later recall. As Socrates said, things "leave their head." He pointed out that a piece of writing does not respond to questions, as do people in conversations. "If you ask a piece of writing a question, it remains silent," he said. Writing is also static: It does not change its mind. Anyone can take a piece of writing and do anything he wants with it, Socrates argued, because writing "has no parent to protect [it]." There is no concept of forgery in oral cultures.

Socrates's antiwriting position reminds us that with writing comes loss. We lose the body. We lose gestures. Without technology we lose some capacity to remember, for a pen is as much a technology as a computer is. We also lose those little phrases injected into speech that individualize us—"those scraps of language" like "Isn't that right?" or "Make sense?"*3

---

* Today, people are inventing new ways to reinsert gestures and individuality into writing. These are often noted with alarm, often by those who also decry the atrophying of handwriting. Think of the

Socrates's words also remind us that oral cultures are no less sophisticated than literate ones. Many of Western civilization's greatest figures never or rarely wrote. What we know about Moses, Buddha, and Jesus all comes from words they spoke, not wrote. Jesus is only described writing once: words in sand he later erased and that no one recorded (John 8:8).

But while they are no less sophisticated, oral cultures are significantly different from literate ones. "Sustained thought in an oral culture is tied to communication."[4] In other words, to think deeply and complexly requires one to talk to someone else.

Thus, oral cultures developed complex, intricate systems for how to remember ideas and then communicate them to others—ways of thinking unavailable to minds that have been altered by becoming literate. A member of an oral culture like Socrates had a capacity for memory that far outstripped his literate counterparts. Since no one could "look up" anything, oral cultures developed elaborate

---

rise in the use of Internet slang like "XO" ("hugs and kisses") and acronyms like "IRL" ("in real life"), and the interest in new, shorter writing forms, like Twitter or the appropriately named "chat" rooms, which are based more on patterns of oral speech than they are on writing. These appeal to people because they offer ways to reinject into writing the individualizing, self-branding scraps of language like "Make sense?" to get writing closer to that Socratic ideal of two people, IRL, having a conversation.

mnemonics, or memory systems, and used additive structures (and ... and ... and) and listing to create memorable rhythms. The book of Genesis, which was originally orally transmitted and later written down, is such an example:

> In the beginning God created heaven and earth. And the earth was void and empty, and darkness was upon the face of the deep; and the spirit of God moved over the waters. And God said: Be light made. And light was made. And God saw the light, that it was good; and he divided the light from the darkness. And he called the light Day, and the darkness Night; and there was evening and morning one day.[5]

The frequent use of "and" makes the structure easy to memorize. Lists are another way to remember: God says light, light is good, light is divided from darkness, light becomes day, dark becomes night.

The Greeks also invented "memory palaces," mnemonic devices in which a speaker would prepare a speech by imagining a palace or other structure he knew well. He would mentally "walk" through each room in the palace, tying a part of the speech to that room: in the foyer, the introduction; on the second-floor balcony, the fifth reason for his argument. For longer, more elaborate speeches, he would mentally place items in each room to signal an idea: the table in the foyer, for example, indicated an aside to be made during the introduction. Using a memory palace, a Grecian orator could lecture for hours. The poet Simonides of Ceos, it is said, attended a party in a house that was then destroyed by an earthquake. Afterward he helped name and recover each victim because he remembered every person who was there, and where he or she lay buried.

While the Greeks respected speaking over writing, and their education focused on rhetorical skills, not fine motor ones, ironically they also invented the most revolutionary technology in the history of writing: the alphabet. This remarkably efficient system was invented only once in history, and it has only one name, regardless of language.

The earliest alphabet was invented sometime around the fifteenth century B.C.E. by Semites living in Canaan, in modern-day Israel, Lebanon, and Jordan, and then spread along the Mediterranean coast. An alphabet is a writing system that uses symbols for sounds rather than syllables or logograms; each sound is represented by one letter. The early Phoenician alphabet represented only consonants; the first alphabet to represent both consonants and vowels is the twenty-two-letter Greek system, developed around 750 B.C.E.; the Latin alphabet derives from the Greek, with additions and modifications from Etruscan. Any alphabet is less cumbersome than previous writing systems: Compare our twenty-six letters to cuneiform and Egyptian hieroglyphs, which both included several thousand signs at points in their development. In addition, alphabets, with their ordering of letters, allow for easier record keeping and lists.

Who actually invented the alphabet is unknown. The legend Greeks told about the origin of the alphabet was that it was brought to them by Cadmus, a Phoenician prince. Whether or not there was an "alphabet inventor," the alphabet was the first conscious analysis of all components of speech broken into constituent parts, and it is the world's most efficient way to represent spoken sounds.

Writing had actually existed in Greece before the alphabet, in Crete during the fifteenth century B.C.E.: Linear A and B were cuneiform-based writing systems (Linear A has yet to be decoded), and the Greeks used them for recording bureaucratic and military matters. But then, for a reason unknown to us now, they put writing aside. Writing in Greece largely disappeared between the twelfth and eighth centuries B.C.E., a period now called the Greek "dark ages," although it was an extraordinarily literate time in which cultural knowledge was vaunted. This is the time of Homeric epics, which were known by every educated Greek. No one knows if Homer was a person; he may have been a collection of bards, or the word "Homer" may just be a shorthand term for a long poem. Whatever the truth, and despite having writing, no one wrote Homer's poems down for generations. Instead, they recited them, memorized them, and recited them again.

Eventually, of course, the ancient Greeks integrated writing into their lives. For their writing surfaces, the Greeks learned from Egyptians how to make papyrus. Greek papyrus was never as elegant as the Egyptian goods though, and Grecian scrolls were always smaller than the twenty-foot-long ones used in Egypt. In fact, the size of Greek scrolls, and the specifics of papyrus, helped determine subsequent literary forms and practices we still use. A play, for example, was usually the length of one Greek scroll. When the *Iliad* and the *Odyssey* were written down, they were divided into "books" that may have originally been determined by the length of a scroll.[6] The beginning of a scroll was called the "protocol," a term which echoes in our prologues, and the side of the papyrus on which the lines naturally run horizontally—and thus is easier to write on, as if it were organically ruled paper—was called the "recto," a term still used by printers.

As a writing tool, a Greek would use a reed pen called a calamus that improved on the Egyptian one by being harder and thicker. Scribes would trim the pen with a knife and split the nib for better ink flow. Alphabetic letters are better written with a sharper point than are hieroglyphs, which are better made with a brushwork motion. Like the Egyptians, Greeks also used ink from ground lampblack (the remains produced when something burns without sufficient air), gum, and water. A knife for trimming the pen, a pumice stone for smoothing the papyrus, and a sponge for erasing completed the Greek scribal tools.

Ancient Greeks didn't use margins when writing, nor were there spaces between the words. Letters were uniformly written, but nothing indicated when a word or sentence or paragraph ended, and no punctuation was employed, because most Greeks spoke the words aloud as they read them. Silent reading and punctuation were still centuries away.

Unlike the Sumerians, whose clay tablets we have today in abundance, or the Egyptians, who buried their papyrus in tombs, the ancient Greeks did not manage to preserve their writing for posterity. We have almost no extant original papyrus documents written in ancient Greek. Most Greek correspondence, bureaucratic records, and original literary works are lost. We do, however, have much evidence of the writing they did on more durable surfaces, such as stone walls, pottery, and gems. And we have, of course, the texts of ancient Greek writing that were deemed important enough that they were subsequently copied.

If the Greeks gave us the alphabet, we owe the Romans for the shape of our Western letters. Ours is the Latin or Roman alphabet—a tweaked version of the Greek, and the transformation of the Greek alphabet to the Roman one was eventually adopted for dozens of languages, thanks to the long history of the Roman Empire and its conquests. The Romans wrote a lot, and their writings are still foundational and well-known to us thousands of years later. But curiously, as with ancient Greece, we know less about how Romans actually wrote—how they taught writing and the methods they used—than we know about how the Sumerians and Egyptians set down their words.

In fact, not until 1748—thousands of years after they were written—was much of the Roman handwriting available to us now discovered in an area called Civita. Archaeologists found remarkably well-preserved documents in the form of graffiti and, to a lesser extent, papyrus in the rubble of Pompeii that was buried in volcanic ash after the eruption of Mount Vesuvius more than a millennium and a half earlier, in 79 B.C.E. Archaeologists started digging—and they have continued to dig for hundreds of years; indeed, one third of the city is yet to be uncovered.

When it comes to preserving handwriting, entombment in volcanic ash rivals firing clay and burying papyrus. The best-preserved examples in Pompeii are graffiti found inside houses and on the walls of buildings. Some three thousand examples of political campaigning have been found, written in either red or black. Most simply include a name, the position the person was running for, and maybe a note like "worthy of public office."[7] Also found were many profane writings by individuals, and they, not surprisingly, give us more insight into average Romans who were as concerned with ribald and scatological references as today's graffiti writers are. "Weep, you girls. My penis has given you up. Now it penetrates men's behinds. Goodbye, wondrous femininity!" wrote someone on the wall of a bar and brothel. In a bathhouse, a man named Severus wrote: "Successus, a weaver, loves the innkeeper's slave girl named Iris. She, however, does not love him. Still, he begs her to have pity on him. His rival wrote this. Goodbye."[8] With ancient graffiti, the power of writing to simply attest to one's presence on earth is over-powering, as emotive as it is to hold a cuneiform tablet in the palm of one's hand.

A trove of graffiti was discovered in what was the ancient Greek city of Smyrna (present-day Izmir, Turkey) in 2013. We have many pieces of ostraca, the "scratch paper of the ancient world,"[9] those shards of clay so many cultures wrote on. And the Vindolanda tablets, discovered in 1973 on the site of a Roman garrison in northern England, are small wooden letters dating to the first and second centuries C.E. containing military documents and personal messages; these are the oldest surviving examples of Roman ink writing. Romans also apparently wrote on bark, because we have comments about this in Pliny the Elder and elsewhere. Although there are no extant examples of bark writing, the Latin word for "bark" comes from *liber*, the word we use for book, and that also forms the root of Latin words for both "bookseller" and "scribe."

But precious little Roman writing on papyrus has been

found. Most of what we have comes from one thousand partial scrolls, almost all written by the philosopher and poet Philodemus of Gadara, found in Herculaneum. However, the contents of many important Roman texts have been preserved because the early Christian church set up veritable factories to copy and recopy them.*

Romans also used wax tablets, which were made by scraping out the insides of a piece of wood or ivory to create a bed, then filling it with wax. When two pieces of wood or ivory were joined together, the tablet was called a diptych; for three a triptych (as similarly constructed paintings are named). Romans jotted things down on their tablets and then erased them to write something new. The Roman stylus, also a calamus, had one sharper end for writing, and another, broader end for erasing. Unlike scrolls, tablets were easier to transport and were used for documents, letters, and school assignments. Some wax tablets even had writing on the outside, summarizing the text inside, much like the flap copy of a book.

The Romans were avid writers, producing thousands of administrative documents backed up by many laws, and each Roman colony had its own written constitution. The extremely complex Roman bureaucracy produced a need

---

* Similarly, I do not know where the original file of a word-processed article I wrote in 1999 might be found, but I have paper copies of it in a file cabinet.

for many documents. The Romans were also more interested in writing down their histories, rather than orally transmitting them like the Greeks.

But Roman writing was not all laws and history. They also liked to curse, and they created "curse tablets" exclusively for this purpose. One was discovered a few years ago in England, far from the capital, having lain undiscovered for centuries because it had been hidden in what was then likely a temple. Romans wrote the names of those they were cursing upside down; the curses themselves, like the graffiti found in Pompeii, are both hilariously resonant and startlingly unfamiliar, such as the prayer that a victim "become as liquid as water" or that "I curse Tretia Maria and her life and mind and memory and liver and lungs mixed up together, and her words, thoughts and memory; thus may she be unable to speak what things are concealed."[10]

Romans were influenced by the Greeks in all facets of writing, from the way it was taught to how it was written. As in Greece, orality still carried enormous influence and prestige in politics and the law. Writing was done by minions, not by emperors and statesmen themselves, so the famous and wellborn orated while scribes recorded their words. Some of those scribes were Greeks who had been enslaved. Julius Caesar is said to have had seven scribes; one imagines an entourage of scribblers following him as he strode into the Coliseum.

We owe much of what we know about Roman events to scribes. For example, Pliny the Elder, the philosopher and commander of the Roman military, was on the Bay of Naples in the summer of 79 A.D. Noticing smoke coming from across the water, he set out on a boat to get a closer look. He took a scribe with him, to whom he dictated what he was seeing. The smoke was the eruption of Mount Vesuvius. As his boat approached the city, the rowers advised Pliny to head back, to which he famously responded, "Fortune favors the brave," and told the helmsmen to keep going. They made land at Pompeii, which they found "in the greatest consternation." They were unable to get back into the boat and leave, but Pliny encouraged the party to wait it out and then, at some point—perhaps due to inhaling gases—collapsed and died. The rest of the group survived. When they returned home, the scribe gave his notes to Pliny the Younger, who then rewrote his uncle's words.

To the Romans we owe not just our alphabet but our first books. Roman books were made by trimming pieces of papyrus to the same size, tying them together, and putting them between boards. Some credit Julius Caesar as being the first to fold a roll of papyrus into pages instead of a scroll, but the first reference to the "book" as we know it today comes from the poet Martial, who lived from about 38 to 102 C.E.:

Whoa, that's enough now,
whoa, little book!
We've come now right
to the end.
You're keen to keep
going any further,
And you can't be held
back on the last page,
As if you hadn't finished
the task
That was finished already
on the first page.
Now your reader is
grumbling and giving up,
Now even the scribe
himself is saying
"Whoa, that's enough now,
whoa, little book!"[11]

Romans eventually shifted from papyrus to parchment, and this made books even more convenient. Papyrus had to be imported from Egypt. Parchment, made from animal skins, could be locally produced. By the first century B.C.E., bookstores had been established in Rome and other cities such as Carthage, Lyon, and Brindisi, selling both new and used books. The first X-rated and pulp books, as well as fine literary works, were published. And the wealthy started collecting the new technology into libraries.

The book did not kill the scroll any more than writing killed speech. But the classical veneration of orality is as important if not more so to understanding Greek and Roman civilization as are their writings. Eventually, writing as a form of communication, and the codex book as the privileged form of its transmission, would become the bedrock forms of transmitting Western knowledge. And from late antiquity through the medieval era in Europe, the work of transmission—of reproducing bound sheaves of pages—fell to lowborn monks laboring in dark, drafty monasteries.

Chapter 4

HUMAN XEROX MACHINES

W̲E̲ ̲O̲W̲E̲ ̲M̲U̲C̲H̲ of our knowledge of Greek and
Roman thought to the early Christians, who
copied their texts, over and over, in gorgeous, regimented
handwriting.[1] These intricate manuscripts may indeed
represent the apogee of handwriting in the West. Those
who wrote them were primarily monks tasked with
working for hours on end. They were not laboring under
our modern notions of writing as expression; writing for
them was neither creative nor original. The scribal monk's
goal was, in fact, to eradicate any sign of personality and
produce multiple copies of the same books. Human copying
machines of sorts, medieval scribes proved that handwriting
does not, in and of itself, reveal personality or the self.

Being a monastic scribe was not a particularly high-
ranking position, although the work was important

enough that one Irish law punished the murder of a scribal monk as harshly as the murder of a bishop or even a king. Scribal monks were usually from poor families or men who held strong religious convictions. Scribes were valued, as their products were important to the prestige of the monastery: Their workplace was usually set up in a place that was difficult to attack, should an enemy appear, such as an upper floor. But they were not exalted as scribes were in Egypt; nobles and high-ranking church members, as in Rome, dictated their words to these lesser others. Orality was still far more appreciated than writing in the early medieval era, both as rhetorical skill and as the primary form of communication.

Scribes took dictation for church business, but that was not as laborious as the more important job of making copies of key religious, philosophical, and historical works, which they would do in a scriptorium, the suitably factory-sounding term for the room inside a monastery where monks sat to do their copying. Many classical texts were not deemed worthy of copying in the first centuries after the fall of Rome and were thus lost, but some were preserved by Byzantines and Muslims, as well as individual Christians who valued classical learning, such as Boethius, and a few monasteries, such as those in Ireland, that copied Roman texts. By copying and recopying, the scribes helped Christianity spread across Europe; over centuries, books were brought to monasteries and then copied again by another set of monks.

The labor involved in handwriting a book was intensive. A medieval scribe made his own pens from goose or swan feathers, preferably ones from the bird's outer left side, as outer feathers were the longest, and the left-side feathers tilted to the right, an angle preferred by monks, who were right-handed by nature or training. Removing the barbs, he would scrape the center spine clean, fashioning a tip by cutting one end of the point at an angle and cutting a slit through it so the shaft could pick up ink. The slit would often open up, and he would use his knife to cut off, re-angle, and re-slit his pen several times an hour. Quill pens did not last long, so he would have to do this process over and over. A typical monk might go through sixty pens in a day.[2] Scribes in the medieval era used two hands, one holding the pen, the other the knife they needed to continually sharpen and re-angle their instrument. Monks held their pens with three fingers "extended or slightly curved" (*tres digiti scribunt*) and two tucked in. The hand rested completely on the little finger; the pen was held almost perpendicular to the paper.

The inks the scribes used were usually made from lamp-black mixed with water and either lye or gum. Red ink was used for headings and the first letter of a word. Making red ink was no easy task, as in this description from Theophilus

Presbyter, an eleventh-century author of a text on the medieval arts, makes clear:

> To prepare white-flake, get some sheets of lead beaten out thin, place them dry in a hollow piece of wood and pour in some warm vinegar or urine to cover them. Then, after a month, take off the cover and remove whatever white there is, and again replace it as at first. When you have a sufficient amount and you wish to make red lead from it, grind this flake-white on a stone without water, then put it in two or three new pots and place it over a burning fire. You have a slender curved iron rod, fitted at one end in a wooden handle and broad at the top, and with this you can stir and mix this flake-white from time to time. You do this for a long time until the red lead becomes visible.[3]

After the feather plucking and slit making and ink preparing, a scribe still needed to create a writing surface. Throughout the medieval era, that was usually made from parchment, and took weeks to prepare. Parchment, or vellum, is made from animal skin. After an animal—a sheep or a goat, usually—was killed, the skin would be removed and the hair and fur washed off. Then the skin was treated with lime to clean it. After that, it was washed repeatedly to remove the lime, scraped clean with an iron, and stretched on a frame to dry. After this process the two sides would be quite different. The inner side, which had been next to the animal's flesh, was called the "recto" The "verso," or back, which used to be next to the fur, was used for the backs of pages. Because animal skin has several layers, an error could be scraped off, another use for that handy left-handed knife. Usually a monk also had a stone on his desk to smooth out the parchment.

Having crafted a page, the monk would rule it, creating horizontal guidelines to keep his letters straight as he wrote across the page, and vertical ones, margins, to make sure the lines didn't drift too far to the top, the bottom, or the edge. He sat at a sloping desk to accommodate the angle of the pen.

Now ready to write, the monk had to sit and write for at least six hours a day. Monks were not allowed candles to keep them warm, for fear of fire. The monk who ran the scriptorium, the *armarius*, told the scribe what to copy each day. Accuracy was essential: Monasteries staked their reputations on how accurate their copies were. An *armarius* sometimes quizzed a scribe on the contents of the book he was copying—called the exemplar—to make sure he understood the text's meaning. It was tedious, slow work. A typical monk spent some three months—all day, every day—copying one book. Since the world was still primarily oral, the convention, until around the ninth century, was to speak while reading. As a monk wrote on one of his manuscripts, "No one can know what efforts are demanded. Three fingers write, two eyes see. One tongue speaks, the entire body labors."[4]

We are not sure exactly when silent reading developed, but in his *Confessions*, Saint Augustine described being shocked to find his friend, Ambrose, reading without saying the words out loud. The move from spoken to silent reading, like so much in this history, took a very long time, as the culture gradually moved from being primarily oral to being more text based. The expression *Verba volent, scripta manent* indicates that speech moves and continues but writing stays in place. Aristotle, updating Socrates to some degree, said that letters were "invented so that we might be able to converse even with the absent."[5] Writing conventions of the time show this continued assumption of orality from ancient times, as medieval scribes also did not use spaces between words, punctuation, or paragraphs. Those are elements that enhance the reading experience but are not required in talking, and were only invented once people became habituated to reading.

Once silent reading became the norm, the scriptoria went quiet. The Church started using silence as a form of devotion and discipline, and to this day many monasteries require absolute silence. Gone were the low mumbles of words being recited for memorization from exemplars. And if a monk needed something—more ink or parchment—he would use hand signals to indicate his needs to the *armarius*. If he needed a new book to work on, he would turn over a page in the air. Sometimes the signals were humorous. If he was copying a Roman book, then considered a pagan text, he would pretend to be a dog and scratch his body, because pagans were regarded as dogs.[6]

Although the work of the medieval scribe was routine drudgery, the books the monks produced are glorious: Looking at them provides a rare aesthetic experience. While their beauty was in part the result of an extremely hierarchical, rigid society, and although individual monks were never recognized, some did smuggle in bits of individuality. There are manuscripts in which a monk either broke a rule to insert himself into the book, or fixed a mistake and left his mark by so doing. In one manuscript, for example, a passage had been left out. The scribe caught the mistake, wrote the missing passage in the margin of the page, and then drew around it a scene showing it being lifted up to the correct spot in the text.

Other scribes left feisty and hilarious comments hidden in margins and back pages, such as this warning to anyone tempted to steal the manuscript: "If anyone take away [i.e. steal] this book, let him die the death; let him be fried in a pan; let the falling sickness and fever seize him; let him be broken on the wheel and hanged. Amen." Others commented on their unending work:

"Here ends the second part of the title work of Brother Thomas Aquinas of the Dominican Order; very long, very verbose, and very tedious for the scribe."

"Thin ink, bad parchment, difficult text."

"Thank God, it will soon be dark."

"Now I've written the whole thing. For Christ's sake give me a drink."[7]

Later in the medieval era, the dominance of the scriptoria weakened, literacy became less restricted, and opportunities for secular scribes and non-monastic bookmaking arose. By the thirteenth century, schools and universities had been founded, and they created new centers of manuscript production. Bookshops and stationers opened, and individuals who were neither nobles nor high-ranking Church members started buying books, just as they had in Roman times. The professional scribe, who had not been needed since Roman times, became a new career opportunity.

Professional scribes were paid by the job, so the faster they could write, the more they could make. One scribe in particular, Giovanni Marco Cinico of Parma, was said to be able to copy a book in fifty-two hours and was nicknamed "Velox," or "Speedy."[8] Scribes could advertise their prowess: The first English advertisement for a scribe was a specimen page showing all the hands he could offer for your book. You could walk into his shop in London and choose your script from among the options. Scribes were also hired by students in the new schools and universities to copy their textbooks, and students lacking funds for an entire book would order their required reading one gathering, or *pecia*, at a time. A gathering refers to the number of pages held together by a fastener (in this case, rope); today, we use the term "signature"—one very correlated with handwriting—to denote this same gathering of pages for a printer. As the semesters progressed, students would return for more *peciae*.

By the fourteenth century, a good number of lay scribes were traveling through towns across Europe, selling their services, showing potential customers sample books, and being hired by students and the wealthy alike. Some began to set up workshops with other craftsmen, which led them to organize into guilds. What was once an act of anonymous religious devotion was slowly transformed into an individual craft as people moved from a feudal to an early capitalist society.

As in the monastery, the guilds required a phalanx of skilled workers to make one book. In the fourteenth century, people were ordering books customized to order, somewhat like ordering a high-end handbag or wedding invitation. The customer would decide on the shape of the book—how large the pages would be, how embellished the cover, how many illustrations—and what contents he wanted. The shop might stock some originals for the customer to peruse. Then the bookseller would hire a scribe, as well as an illustrator, to make the book. Eventually the number of skilled trades related to bookmaking increased to include limners, who drew the pictures; tornours, who drew the initial letters and the borders; rubricators, who colored the red letters; flourishers, who did the curlicues in the margins; parchmenters, who made the parchment; and bookbinders, who sewed the *peciae* together.[9] After the book was done, more specialists, called correctors, would go over the book and point out errors. A seven-year apprenticeship was necessary to become a master in any of these trades.

But being able to leave the monastery and work for oneself did not improve the rank of scribes. Lay scribes were no more vaunted than were the scriptoria laborers who worked for God's glory instead of wages. A professional scribe earned about what a farmhand did, and the work was almost as physical: "It makes the eyes misty, bows the back, crushes the ribs and belly, brings pain to the kidneys, and makes the body ache all over," as one scribe lamented.[10]

Scribal monks sublimated their individuality to authority; the books they wrote were unoriginal copies. But the manuscripts do not all look the same, as the scripts monks used changed many times from late antiquity to the Renaissance. Each script, while very prescribed, was distinct from others, and each one carried a particular connotation. Looked at chronologically, these scripts tell a story of change in Europe from Rome to the Renaissance.

Chapter 5

THE POLITICS OF SCRIPT

SCRIPTS IN THE medieval era symbolized state power or religious authority. At first, the idea that a script could be political or the basis of judgment might seem absurd, but we make similar, if lower-stakes, associations between how letters are formed and the person forming them now. Consider how many perceive people who use the Comic Sans font or the hipster cool of Helvetica. European scripts, from the fall of Rome to the invention of the printing press, were not neutral; they carried great symbolic power.

The first medieval script was borrowed from Rome. The Romans wrote only in capitalis, whether on an obelisk, building, or scroll. The most famous example of this all-capital letter script is Trajan's Column, with its symmetrical and geometric letters. Many consider it to be the most perfect alphabetic script.

The early Christians used Roman square capitals, also called capitalis, for their most important manuscripts. The only remaining manuscripts written in Roman square capitals are from Virgil manuscripts of the fourth and fifth century B.C.E. (We have many more examples on Roman columns and monuments.)[1] The Christians quickly moved away from this script, though, because it was too expensive; Roman square capitals take up a lot of space on the page, and parchment was a valuable commodity, one that did not last long in humid Italy. So they developed a more concentrated script, capitalis rustica, that squeezed each letter. It was a skinny version of capitalis, and was considered a way to save both stone and parchment. Like capitalis, from which the term "capital letters" comes, all rustica letters were capitals.*

Rustica was used from the first to the ninth century, and most frequently in the fourth and fifth centuries; about fifty such manuscripts have survived. It was written in the exact same way, with identical curves and the letters thinned to

---

* Note that the words "uppercase" and "lowercase" make no sense when discussing Roman and medieval script, because those terms come from printing technology: Typesetters put the capitals, or majuscule letters, in cases on top of the minuscules, then the term for "lowercase letters."

precisely the same size. So exact was the writing that it is hard to distinguish a first-century rustica manuscript from one in the fourth century.*

But as Christianity distanced itself from the paganism of Rome, it decided its own rustica script looked too heathen. Around the sixth century, rustica was largely retired, and the Church created what it deemed the Christian-looking uncial. By the start of the fifth century, most scribes across Europe had learned the new script, as some traveled to study the script and returned to teach it to their brothers.[2]

If capitalis still looks Roman to us now, uncial looks medieval, and indeed uncial-influenced fonts are used today for medieval-themed carnivals and fairs, albeit with punctuation that was not invented in the medieval era. Uncial had a long run and remained the most common script through the eighth century, mirroring the Church's spread throughout Europe, and the script came to symbolize consolidation.

Uncial was the primary script but not the only one used at the time: In the fifth century, another script was invented to increase writing speed—a cursive of sorts called half-uncial. This was the first time minuscule (or lowercase) letters were introduced. Saint Augustine wrote

---

* By comparison, distinguishing the handwriting in a letter written in 2014 from that written in 1714 is easy.

in half-uncial, largely because it allowed him to write faster. Uncial and half-uncial were never mixed; you either wrote in ALLCAPTIALUNCIAL or allminusculehalfuncial.

In addition to half-uncial, other secondary scripts sprang up as the Church, and Romance languages, grew. Later termed "national hands" by paleographers even though they overlapped, these scripts signal regional differences: Merovingian was mainly used by the French, Visigothic by the Spanish, Lombardic by the Italians, etc. The most beautiful of these hands may well be Insular, developed in Ireland by Saint Patrick, who had learned half-uncial in Europe and brought it to Ireland in the latter half of the fifth century.

Irish monks embellished half-uncial, made it majuscule, and decorated the initial letters with impossibly intricate designs, creating a distinct hand. The gorgeous, jewel-like Book of Kells was written in Insular, and it may be the most beautiful example of all medieval writing.

Localized and expressive scripts added diversity to manuscripts, but they also made books harder to read for those not trained in a particular hand. Although all books were written in Latin, many people could not read scripts from different regions. Words were made incomprehensible to people who spoke the same language because the letters were written so differently.*

---

* One of the most common concerns many have about the dying of handwriting in the twenty-first century is the loss of history. "How

Documentary hands—or chancery hands—are yet another story in the history of medieval writing. These were developed for government and church business, and are a form of cursive that can be very quickly written. They tend to illegibility today, and few are the scholars who can transcribe their contents. There are only a handful of these manuscripts remaining, making a genealogy of cursive scripts hard to reconstruct.

---

can you read cursive if you cannot write it?" the question usually goes. The truth is, most of us already cannot read 99 percent of the historical record. Nor have people been able to read what has been written during their own lifetimes.

Much handwriting is so hard to read that some people spend years training to read certain scripts, learning a field of study called paleography. Paleographers, however, are not trained to learn all scripts. They specialize. For instance, Heather Wolfe, curator of manuscripts at the Folger Shakespeare Library, is an expert in English secretary hand, the script used for writing documents and letters in England between the sixteenth and eighteenth centuries. Wolfe would find it hard to read the scripts that Carin Ruff, a paleographer of the Cleveland Park Historical Society in Washington, D.C., specializes in, those of early medieval England. Some paleographers are experts in German scripts of the fourth and fifth century, or Latin scripts during the Roman era. Paleographers do not study writing on stone; that is another specialty, called epigraphy. Nor do paleographers study all the scripts of one time. Ruff is an expert on book hands (the scripts used to write manuscript books) of the medieval era, but she knows very little about documentary hands (the scripts used to write charters and other bureaucratic documents) of the same time. In other words, even someone whose life's work is dedicated to reading cursive cannot read most cursive.

This baroque explosion of geographically based scripts from the sixth to the ninth century was an aesthetic and diversifying boon, but to Church leaders it was seen as a form of insubordination, a refusal to adhere to central authority. To consolidate his power, to make the Church more centralized and less locally controlled, Charlemagne, the first emperor of the Holy Roman Empire, who ruled over most of Western Europe in the early ninth century—and is thought to have been illiterate—issued a decree that everyone use the same script he developed called Carolingian minuscule. Like its namesake, Carolingian minuscule conquered Europe and became the authoritative script in France, Germany, Northern Italy, and, eventually, England for two hundred years, from the ninth to the eleventh century.

Not surprisingly, Carolingian minuscule is uniform and standard. The shift to Carolingian minuscule shows, literally, a Church focused on legibility and practicality. Not coincidentally, it looks much like the earlier, Roman-influenced capitalis and capitalis rustica, as Charlemagne was consciously signaling a return to the classical roots of the Church. Centuries earlier, Roman-inspired scripts were connected to paganism, but Charlemagne was inspired by the early years of the Church. Thus, as uncial was developed to distinguish Christian from Roman texts, Carolingian was developed to reconnect the two.

Previous scripts, all with their discrete connotations, were preserved throughout the medieval era through an elaborate organization most often used on title pages of books called by contemporary scholars a "hierarchy of scripts." For instance, a manuscript written in the Carolingian period might have the top line of a title page written in capitalis to show homage to the early Church; rustica for incipits, or the opening words; uncial for chapter headings, tables of contents, and the first line of each new chapter; and half-uncials for prefaces and second lines of text. The text itself would be written in Carolingian minuscule, the reigning script of the time.

Gothic script, or blackletter, which is commonly associated with medieval writing today, evolved as a variation of Carolingian minuscule during the twelfth century. Gothic compresses letters more tightly together. It is more illegible than most scripts, signaling the Church's return to the diversity and localization of the pre-Carolingian period. Gothic is more of a family of scripts than a singular hand; dozens of variations were used across Europe until the invention of the printing press.

Italian scribes were never enamored with Gothic, which did not have the same reach as Carolingian minuscule (Petrarch found Gothic script to be "as though it had been designed . . . for something other than reading"[3]), and in the fifteenth century a new script—clearer, and simpler, and more legible to many—was developed (or, according to some, invented by one man, Poggio Bracciolini).[4]

This script was humanist, a fairly faithful reinvention of Carolingian minuscule, itself a reinvention of capitalis. So severe was the rollback to Rome that distinguishing humanist from Carolingian minuscule, a then seven-hundred-year-old script, is difficult. It was not an easy switch to make: It required a concentrated effort to revive a script that had languished for centuries.

The humanists—Renaissance men seeking to revive classical learning, and realizing that for centuries some monks had been preserving classical texts in scriptoria by copying manuscripts in varying scripts—traveled across Europe looking for the best examples of Roman manuscripts. We know now that almost none survived, but some found what they thought were Roman manuscripts, only to discover later that they were actually ninth-century manuscripts done in Carolingian minuscule, the script created to emulate Roman script. That a book produced nine hundred years later could be confused with a Roman codex makes clear just how stable the production of writing had been during this period.

Humanist script took away the ligatures that connected the letters in Gothic, and used more space between letters than Gothic did. It also abandoned the in-the-know abbreviations used by Gothic scribes, and spelled out entire words. Humanist, as it were, let the air into handwriting; it was, in its references to humanism, accessibility, and classical culture, very much part of the Renaissance.

Stanley Morison, English type designer and historian of printing, argues the reason Gothic looked "barbarous" to humanists was rooted in Cosimo de' Medici's preference for humanist. Medici, to assert his power vis-à-vis the Vatican, wrote in a different hand. Morison uses "roman" to refer to humanist script:

> The [Italics] invented and espoused by the Florentine humanists would never have been established but for the use and support given it by Cosimo de' Medici, who bestowed upon it a quasi-authority. It was essentially different from that of the papal or Imperial chanceries. It is the only example of a script being established because of the accident that it corresponded with the taste of a merchant banker. Without him the then novel script would never have been more than the hobby of a society of 'literati'. In this sense the humanistic roman may be described as a capitalist script.[5]

In his 1528 book on how to correctly pronounce Greek and Latin, *De recta Graeci et Latini sermonis pronunciatione*, the humanist Desiderius Erasmus Roterodamus (Erasmus of Rotterdam) wrote a dialogue between two schoolboys, Ursus and Leo, in which Gothic script is called "bad handwriting" with the "same drawbacks as incorrect pronunciation":

Write out a speech of Cicero's in Gothic script and you will say it is outlandish and barbarous. It either loses its elegance when so written, or the reader completely rejects it or is utterly worn out . . . On the other hand, you would hardly believe how much your material can be set off to advantage by elegant, clear and legible writing when the Latin words are represented in the Latin script.[*]

Elsewhere in the dialogue, Erasmus wrote his own history of handwriting. As the two talk, Erasmus defines what he considered the best way to write letters: exactly as they were written in Trajan's Column, that always-rediscovered exemplar of exemplars:

URSUS: For common scribes with their curves, joins, tails and similar frivolous strokes, in which they revel out [of] a kind of pride, make writing more difficult, without any compensating advantage whatever. For surely you see how in bygone times the gothic hand was harder to learn than the Latin and how nowadays the French and German hands [are] more difficult than the Italian.

LEO: But the Greeks achieved a cursive style, at least in their minuscule.

---

[*] Latin is the same as humanist script.

URSUS: They succeeded in this as in everything else. But I wish that they had not attempted it. I would much prefer the script not to be disfigured with abbreviations.

LEO: But even the ancient Romans used marks of this kind ... [T]here are people who affect a peculiar script of their own, writing Latin in such a way that it might well look like Greek to an unpracticed eye.

URSUS: Those people you describe should be scorned, not imitated ...

LEO: But what sort of models for handwriting do you particularly commend?

URSUS: The most perfect example of majuscules is on coins struck at the time of Augustus and in the immediately succeeding centuries, especially in Italy; in the provinces the craftsmen owing to lack of experience fell short. For minuscules, Italy everywhere provides the models ...

LEO: On what is the elegance of letters primarily based?

URSUS: On four things: their shape, the way they are joined, their linear arrangement, and their proportion ... Nothing is uglier than ... unevenness.

LEO: Yet this is just how my wife writes!

After making this slur, Leo continues to explain that Gothic is inappropriate for handwriting because it is ugly and barbaric, conflating the quality of one's handwriting with the ability to express oneself, suggesting that one who writes in a barbarous hand is less literate.

Medieval scripts carry cultural meaning: Uncial was designed to distinguish Christianity from Rome, whereas humanist script self-consciously referred back to Christianity's roots in that same Rome. To most of us, humanist is easier to read. And yet we still can see our own prejudices, our own values, in the nodding of heads when we get to this end of the story. We perceive these scripts as clean and legible because we have decided to define "clean" and "legible" along the same lines the humanists did when they invented the script, as did the Romans when they invented theirs. Humanist is easier for us to read because it is more familiar, not because it is intrinsically more legible. One could argue that the triumph of humanist is, ironically, the triumph of standardization. With the invention of the printing press, script could be literally standardized—identically reproduced through fonts.

Chapter 6

HANDWRITING AS DISTINCTION

SINCE MEDIEVAL MONASTERIES were central to the production of writing and books, they were threatened by the prospect of being upended by a new device that some claimed would do the same work faster and better. In his essay *In Praise of Scribes*, the monk Johannes Trithemius made a series of claims against the printing press: "Scripture on parchment can persist a thousand years, but . . . the printed book is a thing of paper and in a short time will decay entirely," he proclaimed, and printed texts would be "deficient in spelling and appearance." "Posterity will judge," he predicted, "the manuscript book superior to the printed book."[1]

Trithemius, like Socrates before him and many who worry about the loss of handwriting today, focused on the same points: The new technology will prove less durable than the old and it will lead to historical amnesia, lesser levels of education, and decreased standards. Unsurprisingly, the most vocal opponents of new technologies are those who dominated the old.

Trithemius was wrong about the durability of print books, but he made another point about handwriting that continues to resonate. Handwriting, he said, was a spiritual act, a form of religious devotion that putting blocks into a press could never be.

Print spread rapidly. Gutenberg's first Bible was printed in 1450; by 1490 there were forty thousand printed books in circulation. By 1600 that number had increased more than tenfold. Martin Luther would complain that "the multitude of books is a great evil. There is no measure or limit to this form of writing."[2] Erasmus regretted that "in former times pupils at school had to take down so much long-hand that boys wrote rapidly but with difficulty, constantly on the look-out for symbols and for abbreviations to save time . . . Nowadays the art of printing has led to the situation that some scholars do not write down anything at all!"

Erasmus's dialogue, published in a printed pamphlet, reminds us that manuscripts persisted after Gutenberg's invention. People did not suddenly get up from their scriptorium desks, throw away their pens, and start pressing type against paper. The two technologies continued side by side. There were hundreds of thousands of (manuscript) books in circulation before Gutenberg's press and, afterward, scores of manuscript books continued to be made.[*]

In fact, the first books, called incunabula, meaning "from the cradle," look identical to manuscript books produced at the same time and were much less revolutionary than Trithemius's words suggest. Seen side by side, the first books and the manuscripts of this period are difficult to distinguish one from the other. To mimic so closely the look of familiar books, early printers had to develop laborious, inefficient processes. For instance, Gutenberg's Bible used red letters at the beginning of each section, as was the practice with manuscripts. This meant each page had to be passed through the press twice and lined up precisely so the red ink appeared in the correct spot. Early printed books included illustrations, often in different colors, so scribes and illustrators were hired to hand-ink a page after it had been printed. Early printed books also included rubrications (additions in red ink), margins, and even guidelines that were standard in scribal manuscripts.

---

[*] It's the same today: For more on this, you can read Sven Birkert's *The Gutenberg Elegies: The Fate of Reading in an Electronic Age* (New York: Faber and Faber, 1994) in print, on the Web, or on your Kindle.

The first font—the print equivalent of a script—also emulated a manuscript. Gutenberg carved into wood a Gothic script that was extremely elaborate, and hired craftsmen to cut and hand-carve the 290 characters needed to print every upper- and lowercase letter, symbol, and punctuation mark so they would look like the ink-drawn versions of the letters scribes were then producing with their pens. This, like the red letters and guidelines, made printed books seem familiar and respectable, easing new readers in. As the future Pope Pius II wrote to Cardinal Carvajel in 1455: "All that has been written to me about that marvelous man seen at Frankfurt [Gutenberg] is true . . . The script was very neat and legible, and not at all difficult to follow; your grace would be able to read it without effort, and indeed without glasses."[*3]

Trithemius and his fellow scribes did ultimately find themselves with less work after printing was introduced. Monks and guildsmen lost a centuries-long monopoly on bookmaking. One scribe, Antonio Sinibaldi, complained

---

[*] Computers and digital books similarly stole from the world of print. We type on "desktops" with "folders" and "files" that we can "cut, copy, and paste," terms borrowed from print culture that helped us conceptualize a new form of writing by comparing it to an older, familiar one. Once we are familiar with the new, the vestiges of the old can be discarded. Printed books eventually abandoned guide-lines, for example, and instead of folders we are using the "cloud."

while doing his taxes that the printing press had taken so much of his business that he had no money for clothes.[4]

The printing press created new professional possibilities for those who were good at handwriting, however. Once facing unemployment, scribes shifted gears. Instead of writing a few commissioned a books year, they started to teach penmanship to others though tutoring, classes, and books. These new writing masters traveled around Europe, and eventually the occupation rose higher in prestige than most scribes ever attained; writing masters became wealthy professionals. The profession of secretary also arose, as the age of exploration and new lands brought on more business and governmental bureaucracy and thus more documents to be written and copied. Secretaries had to take dictation, write documents quickly, and know multiple specialized scripts. A particularly good hand could rise someone above his station. Poggio Bracciolini, the possible inventor of humanist script, had such good handwriting that he ascended from poverty to become papal secretary, one of the highest positions a commoner could obtain in Renaissance Europe. Writing masters also published printed books to disseminate their lessons and, ironically, depended on the distribution printing offered to make their fortunes.

The earliest writing masters mainly taught either italics, a version of humanist, or Gothic, depending upon where they were: The French and Italians preferred italics, whereas Germany and Germanic countries favored Gothic. In England, Queen Elizabeth and King Charles I wrote in italics, which they called Italian chancery hand. This script became associated with the Renaissance, while Gothic came to signify the cloistered Dark Ages. By the sixteenth and seventeenth centuries, wealthy Europeans added additional hands that denoted class, gender, and profession. Men of leisure were taught one hand; clerks wrote in another. Most privileged Europeans used one script for a personal letter and another for a legal document.

Because script needed to signal so many things—the type of document (legal, governmental, business, personal) and the type of writer (noble, professional, lowly, male, female)—and varied from country to country, the history of scripts from the fifteenth to the nineteenth century is a dizzying, arcane, and often confusing one.* Some scripts

---

* There is no logical explanation for the rise of all these different hands; it was a cultural phenomena. To understand, consider how many different website designs or themes are available to someone who wants to set up a site using WordPress. Each one has its own look and its own associations, and when there is no consensus as to how words should look, there is enormous choice. Early in the computer age, people reveled in choosing a different font to best clothe their letters. That has settled down now, as Times New Roman—another "New Roman" script, like Carolingian minuscule and humanist—has become a de facto standard.

were faddish. In England, secretary hand—a cramped, almost illegible script that took hold in the sixteenth century—was widely adopted. Shakespeare used it. By 1525, secretary hand was the most commonly written English script. But one hundred years later it was rarely used, and by 1700 it was considered archaic.

In England, numerous scripts were developed just for court documents, including chancery hand, Common Pleas, and Exchequer Pipe Office, all used by different officials for various purposes. These scripts became increasingly illegible to anyone not trained in that particular sector. For Charles Dickens, these scripts were symbolic. Bob Cratchit, in *A Christmas Carol*, is unable to see his sick child on Christmas because he has to write yet another illegible, unnecessary contract or letter; Lady Honoria Dedlock, in *Bleak House*, is confused by a personal letter written in what appears to be sixteenth-century Chancery hand, a script that was then used exclusively for yet another illegible law hand; a clerk in *The Pickwick Papers* boasts that he can control court proceedings, "since nobody alive except myself can read the [judge's] writing, [and] they [the plaintiffs] are obliged to wait for his opinions . . . till I have copied 'em, ha-ha-ha!"[5]

Compounding the challenge of deciphering the many different hands, no standardized spelling existed in England (or America) until the seventeenth century. Once English supplanted Latin as the language of business and, thus, writing, people wrote down words in any way that sounded the way it was spoken. Shakespeare spelled his name in a number of different ways. Spelling changed during the sixteenth century as literacy became more widespread and people began to be influenced by the spellings they read—and needed to be able to more clearly communicate through written words. Impromptu spellings invented to best reflect speech sounds gradually became codified and standardized. The same applied to punctuation, which had been largely nonexistent or nonstandardized. Not until the eighteenth century did spelling and punctuation become regularized, and only after spelling guides and even more importantly diction-aries first were created and published during the seventeenth century.

From the sixteenth through the nineteenth century, more people learned to read than write. The two skills were generally taught sequentially: Reading came first, and writing was not included in all lessons. Many women were taught to read but then not taught to write. Thus, there were people who could read even though they could not wield a pen. Those lucky women who were taught to write used their own separate-but-not-equal script. In England they did not use the complicated English secretary hands or the various legal hands. Instead, they wrote in what was called Italian hand, a simpler script for the simpler sex. Martin

Billingsley, in a seventeenth-century writing manual, explained women should only be taught Italian hand because "it is conceived to be the easiest hand that is written with Pen, and to be taught in the shortest time: Therefore it is usually taught to women, for as much as they (having not the patience to take any great paines, besides phantasticall and humorsome) must be taught that which they may instantly learn."[6]

Despite the variety of hands, each person was expected to use the hand precisely the same as every other person, looking as close as possible to a copy. Scripts by the eighteenth century no longer represented one's devotion to God or one's proximity to the pope. Instead they showed one's wealth, profession, and breeding.

This was true even in that most individualist of places, the New World. From colonial times through the early decades of the nineteenth century, schooling mainly took place in the home, and boys and girls learned very differently (if they learned at all). Literacy was more restricted, and more gender divided, than many assume. Most people living in New England in the eighteenth century did not know how to write. A higher percentage knew how to read: About 60 percent of men and 30 percent of women were literate. Reading was taught by a woman, usually a mother, so children could read scripture.[7]

Writing, on the other hand, was not usually taught to women at all, and it was taught by men, mainly by writing masters who advertised their services, often for those who wanted to expand their skill set by taking night courses in "Writing and Arithemetick."[8] One master also sold "the best Virginia Tobacco cut, spun into the very best Pigtail . . . also Snuff, at the cheapest Rates."[9] If a girl was taught writing, it was alongside other domestic skills, such as embroidery, music, and dancing. As one maxim in copybooks put it, "Then let the Fingers, whose unrivall'd Skill, Exalts the Needle, grace the Noble Quill."[10]

The first American script, imported from England, was called, appropriately, the *Mayflower* Century Style of American Writing. It combined English secretary hand with a variation of humanist called round hand. Eventually a distinctively American script emerged, called variously round hand or copperplate, with rounded letters and flourishes as well as thin ascenders and thick descenders. It is to this script we owe those odd superscript abbreviations ("W^{m}" for "William") and the long *s*. The Declaration of Independence is written in round hand.

Despite what we were taught, Thomas Jefferson did not pen the Declaration of Independence, at least not the version we have today. Like other wealthy men of the time, he hired a secretary, who had probably been trained by a writing master, to make a fair copy of the draft he wrote. Records show that after the declaration was approved on July 4, the Continental Congress had it engrossed on parchment, and a month later, on August 2, the fair copy was compared to Jefferson's version and signed."[11] No one is sure who engrossed that copy, but it is thought a writing master named Timothy Matlack is responsible for the lettering on view under glass in the National Archives.

In seventeenth-century Boston, some public schools had a writing track, akin to what Americans now call vocational education, for people who wanted to rise in rank by being secretaries. Students spent two years learning scripts: bills of sale, receipts, and legal documents all required different hands. University-bound students enrolled in a different track were taught the round hand of a gentleman.

In the colonies as on the continent, writing masters taught future gentlemen but were not themselves of that rank. Many aimed for such genteel status, and they bristled at those who said teaching penmanship was a mere craft, akin to manual labor. To complicate their desired rise in rank, there emerged a double standard that persists today: The more educated and illustrious you were, the worse your handwriting was supposed to be. Thomas De Quincey said of eighteenth-century French aristocrats that they "ambitiously cultivated a poor hand . . . as if in open proclamation of scorn for the arts by which humbler people oftentimes got their bread."[12] Having a perfect hand could mark one as a parvenu. In what was the final defeat in the attempt to make writing master a lauded profession, writing instruction was feminized. By the 1830s, schools were becoming more common, and they started teaching penmanship as well as reading; female teachers replaced male writing masters as teaching overall became more feminized.

The printing press toppled handwriting off its throne as the de facto way for states and churches to brand themselves through the look of letters, but individuals, with increased access to literacy, were able to take on this role through the heterogeneity of scripts available during this increasingly stratified and bureaucratic time. Eventually, however, individual handwriting was standardized, too. In America, two men developed scripts that would, one after the other, become the universal hand for the nation.

Chapter 7

RIGHTEOUS, MANLY HANDS

GENEVA-ON-THE-LAKE, Ohio, is a tired resort
town on the shores of Lake Erie. It is also the former
home of Platt Rogers Spencer, a true believer in the ennobling qualities of script. Spencer was born in Dutchess
County, New York, in 1800, and moved to Ohio in 1810.
He was the youngest of ten children, raised by his mother
after his father passed away. He was obsessed with penmanship as a child. According to a 1900 encyclopedia entry
(and perhaps backed up only by legend): "Young Spencer
was always passionately fond of penmanship, writing in his
early years upon anything procurable—sand, snow, ice,
brick, bark, the fly-leaves of his mother's Bible, etc., and
by permission of a kind old cobbler, upon the leather in his
shop." By age fifteen he was teaching writing classes,
working as a clerk and studying literature, Latin, and law

as well as penmanship. He taught school and did accounting, but he decided against college when, as the 1900 biography puts it, "The drinking customs, then prevalent in society, proved too strong for him." In 1828 he married Persis Duty, "a lady of remarkable devotion and force of character." She got him sober, and by 1832, Spencer was lecturing on temperance and claimed he was the first American of the century to take a public stand for abstinence from alcohol. He became the Ashtabula County treasurer. He was also a passionate abolitionist and proponent of universal education. With Persis, he fathered eleven children. He was also the first American to create a penmanship franchise, a business that included schools, books, pens, and instructional materials.[1]

Once a year, a workshop called the Spencerian Saga is held on Geneva-on-the-Lake to teach people this script. When he is not teaching the Saga, Michael Sull—Spencer's latter-day heir and America's current leading penman—travels around the country giving Spencerian demonstrations. Spencerian is full of curlicues and swirls. To visualize it, picture the words "Coca-Cola," the ubiquitous brand written on bottles and cans. As the Coca-Cola logo demonstrates, it is an ornate and complicated script not terribly popular today, even among calligraphers hired to write wedding invitations and diplomas. Sull, however, believes Spencerian to be "the most beautiful script in the history of Western Civilization."

Sull's pupils sit at tables learning how to wield steel nibs and make the upward strokes one must make to master Spencerian. One needs the right nib, a small piece of steel, about 1 inch by 1½ with a narrow slit through the middle and a round end for clamping it onto the holder. Holders are pens without tips, pieces of wood carefully hewn to best fit in between fingers. Writing with a nib is confusing and counterintuitive to anyone used to pencils, ballpoints, or felt tip pens. The nib sticks out at an angle from the holder, so one has to hold one's hand further away from the paper, and at a different angle, since the nib is at a 90-degree angle from the pen. The orientation compels you to sit up straighter and hold your arms wider and farther away from your body, and sitting thus one feels slightly different, more upright. Starting with Spencer, no longer was handwriting a way to display one's status; it became a process through which one learned key values. In the second half of the nineteenth century in America, having a good Spencerian hand was an indicator that you were Christian, educated, and proper.

With his knack for public speaking and his quasi-religious zeal for penmanship, Spencer quickly became successful. In 1848 he published a set of exercises, called "copy-slips," together with Victor M. Rice, who then became the superintendent of New York State public schools. From there, Spencer established business colleges to teach his philosophy, "Education for Real Life." The colleges were mainly in the Midwest, and many survive today, teaching workplace skills; some are now run by the for-profit Bryant & Stratton College, with which Spencerian schools were allied from the beginning. Spencerian also became the official government script. For fifty years, Americans would be taught to copy out this one man's invention in order to succeed in school and work.

Spencer's way of making letters became so popular because he imbued his letters with moral and spiritual valences that elevated his system above mere practicality. He used Lake Erie as the basis, so the "true imagery of writing is culled then from the sublime and beautiful in nature." Living during the age of American Transcendentalism—the movement led by writers such as Ralph Waldo Emerson and Henry David Thoreau—Spencer was inspired by nature. He fashioned *a*'s, *b*'s, and *c*'s from the shapes of rocks, branches, and lakes that he looked at every day. The inspiration for his ovals thus came from stone, the branches suggested the linking between letters, and waves lapping on the shore the downstrokes. Sunbeams were straight lines; clouds were curves. As he put it in a poem:

> *Evolved 'mid nature's unpruned scenes,*
> *On Erie's wild and woody shore,*
> *The rolling wave, the dancing stream,*
> *The wild-rose haunts in days of yore.*

The opal, quartz and ammonite,
Gleaming beneath the wavelet's flow,
Each gave its lesson—how to write—
In the loved years of long ago.

Spencer felt that, upon sitting down to write, one should contemplate nature, and the act of writing was noble, genteel work: "It takes Penmanship quite out of the circle of arts merely mechanical" and gives it "dignity as an intellectual pursuit."[2] By elevating penmanship into a moral duty, he also sought to make the teaching of penmanship into a more prestigious, lofty, and intellectual vocation. It was not just about learning one's letters, he told Americans. It was about being a better person.

Spencer also argued that good penmanship could be an engine of social mobility: it "refines our tastes, assists in cultivating our judgment, and thereby makes us better men," said one of Spencer's followers, among the many who used handwriting to rise from penury to the respected position of writing master. Another stated, in a patronizing tone many used, that lessons brought to "cultivated masses . . . a love for beautiful forms and such a facility in producing them as to really elevate and ennoble their thoughts and lives."[3]

Facsimile editions of the 1874 system, reissued by disciples of Spencer in 1985, come in a manila envelope with five copy books to use for the "Theory of Spencerian Penmanship in Nine Easy Lessons." "In every properly conducted school," the instructions begin, "the writing exercise is commenced and closed in an orderly manner: 1. Position at Desk. 2. Arrange Books. 3. Find Copy and Adjust Arms. 4. Open Inkstand. 5. Take Pens . . . At this point the teacher should pay particular attention to giving instruction in pen holding. When ready to write, give the order to TAKE INK." The following page contains detailed instructions on how to sit: "Those who do not wish to become hollow-chested or round-shouldered, should learn to sit easily upright, and keep the shoulders square." Several pages on posture follow before another lesson on how to hold the pen: "Take the pen between the first and second fingers and the thumb, observing, 1st, that it crosses the second finger on the corner of the nail; 2nd, that it crosses the fore finger forward of the knuckle; 3rd, that the end of the thumb touches the holder opposite the lower joint of the fore finger; 4th, that the top of the holder points towards the right shoulder; 5th, that the wrist is above the paper, and the hand resting lightly on the nails of the third and fourth fingers; 6th, that the point of the pen comes *squarely* to the paper." Spencer believed in "whole arm movement." Pupils were trained to use their shoulders and elbows in their letter making.

The rest of the principles provide detailed instruction on how to make each line, stroke, and loop for every letter. There are a total of 196 instructions, posed in question-and-answer form, one of which reads:

Will you explain the construction of small i? Begin on base line and ascend with the right curve, on connective slant, one space; here unite angularly and descend with a straight line on main slant to base; turn as short as possible without stopping the pen, and ascend with a right curve on connective slant, one space. Finishing with a light dot, one space above the straight line on main slant. Note: Directions are best remembered when immediately put in practice. The pupil should trace a model letter a number of times, repeating and following descriptions until the construction is familiar. During such drill the correct position ought to be observed. The exercise may be profitably varied, and easier movements secured by tracing and counting the strokes. Thus, in the small i: 1, 2, 1, dot.

In a turn that recalls the monks in the scriptorium, students were advised to practice their drills six to twelve hours a day, repeating and following descriptions until the construction was familiar. The spiritual values of Spencerian are lost in detailed systemization. Instead of inspiration from nature and Christianity, we get militaristic drilling and are told that, by following these orders, "entire classes may soon be trained to work in concert, all the pupils beginning to write at the same moment, and executing the same letter, and portion of a letter simultaneously."[4]

Despite the grueling, unromantic reality of learning Spencerian, it only became more popular as the years went on. Spencer died in 1864; his last request was for his pen, which he died holding.[5] His message—that by disciplining your hand you could also discipline your mind—kept being impressed upon schoolchildren as more public high schools and business colleges opened.

A. N. Palmer took up Spencer's torch and shaped handwriting in the late nineteenth and early twentieth century. Like Spencer, Palmer was a charismatic true believer. Palmer was born in 1860 and grew up in New York and New Hampshire, where he enrolled in a business college and mastered many scripts from the well-known penman George Gaskell. Palmer then traveled west, teaching penmanship in business colleges, until he took a job with the Iowa Railroad Company and discovered the vast number of documents clerks had to write each day; the workload was too intensive for those Spencerian flourishes and shading. He decided to create a script more suitable for the increased bureaucracy needed by an industrializing country. He also believed his script would improve character, and he demanded that his script be taught by rigid, rote instruction. Palmer's script was adopted by most American schools after they abandoned Spencerian. By the 1920s most Americans had been "Palmerized" and used the Palmer Method.[6]

Palmer disliked Spencerian. He decried it as feminine, fusty, and inefficient for the industrial, energetic America after the Civil War. Spencerian required too much taking up and putting down the pen, and too much shading. The Palmer Method was meant to be an efficient, simple style for the industrial age. It was useful, practical, and business-friendly: Gone were embellishments and flourishes. In 1910 a penmanship supervisor for the Cincinnati schools switched to the Palmer Method because Spencerian was "pretty" but he wanted "real, live, usable, legible, and salable" penmanship.[7]

If Spencer epitomized the Christian moralism of the first half of the nineteenth century, Palmer symbolized the postbellum religion of capitalism. If Spencer thought you could find letter forms by contemplating nature—and that by writing this way you could become more righteous—Palmer believed that muscularity was the key: "If the movement is right, and its application right, the letter will take care of itself." A student needed to perform "sweeping motions of the arm from the shoulder powered by a 'driving force' that was both positive and assertive."[8] Students would learn how to do this by rote repetition: "The letters should be analyzed and studied until the pupil can shut his eyes and see a perfectly formed letter on his eye-lids."[9]

It took weeks, sometimes months, just to get the arm movement right, so students did drills to keep their arms in perpetual motion in order to attain the proper muscle memory. The exercises were "what the gymnasium exercises are to the athlete."[10] One set of instructions used the phrase "writing machine" to refer to the human body, and students practiced arm movements alone for three to six weeks before picking up a pen:

> Do not think of writing or pen holding at this point, but give all your attention to position, muscular relaxation, and the running of the writing machine, until good position and easy movement have become natural.[11]

Palmer even suggested students cut off "the right undersleeve at the elbow" to allow for "unrestricted actions."[12]

As if mimicking the newly established assembly lines adopted at factories during this period of industrialization, the Palmer Method breaks down letters into small constituent parts:

> See how many compact ovals you can make with one dip of ink, and try to develop a motion so light and elastic that you will soon be able to make from five hundred to a thousand, and one thousand or more on a line eight inches long . . . Indeed, one boy of twelve made three thousand [ovals] within the limits of a page eight inches across, maintaining a uniform speed of two hundred to a minute . . .[13]

Like Spencerian, the Palmer Method was advertised as a way to uplift people. But instead of the spiritual religiosity of Spencer, Palmer was more vocational and reform-minded. His script had an "ethical value": "Penmanship training ranks among the most valuable aids in reforming 'bad' children" and is "the initial step in the reform of many a delinquent," he maintained.[14] By learning how to use their arms, "pupils learn . . . that proper conventions must be observed in order to preserve social order and relations." It was said to make immigrants more "American" through its "powerful hygienic effect." Left-handed pupils were forced to use their right hands, for lefties were considered devious.[15]

By 1912, Palmer was a household name, and a million copies of his writing manuals had sold. As the bureaucracy of industrial America piled up, so, too, did the routinized work of clerks, who became "pen pushers" and "quill drivers." Increasingly, women filled these positions. In 1870, business colleges—some founded by Spencer—were mostly attended by men. By 1900 they were predomi-nately female. The popular image of a secretary, assumed to be a man before the turn of the century, became a woman. By 1930, 92 percent of stenographers were women.[16]

The Palmer Method began to lose its predominance in America in the 1930s when mastering this "masculine" script was no longer the way for men to enter middle-class professions and other scripts arose claiming to improve upon it, including Zaner-Bloser, a script similar to Palmer. Zaner-Bloser, which emphasized education and pedagogy more and ornamentalism less, became—and remains—a dominant force not only in elementary education but also in the curriculum materials and handwriting supplies market. The Palmer Method would still be taught by individual teachers throughout the twentieth century, though, and there remain many Americans who were taught the Palmer Method in school, since many elementary school teachers had been trained in it and continued to teach it even after it lost its preeminence.

Students who learned to write in America, from its earliest days through the first half of the twentieth century, were learning a lot more than just their letters. They were learning Christian and national values. With Palmer, efficiency was a key goal. But with the invention of the first machine for individuals to print their writing—the typewriter—even the fastest Palmer writer could not keep up.

Typical cuneiform tablet from the third to second millennium B.C. Musée du Louvre, Paris. GETTY IMAGES

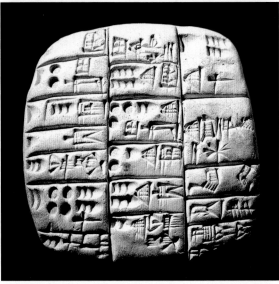

Administrative clay tablet from the third millennium B.C.: cuneiform script showing count of goats and rams from Tell Telloh (ancient Ngirsu), Iraq. GETTY IMAGES

The Edwin Smith papyrus, the world's oldest surviving surgical document.
Written in hieratic script in ancient Egypt around 1600 B.C.

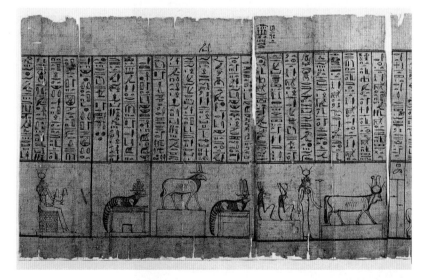

Jumilhac Papyrus, first century B.C.: treaty of mythological geography in
cursive hieroglyphs. GETTY IMAGES

Roman curse tablet discovered in the English city of Bath. PHOTO BY GEMMA SOUTHGATE

SENATVSPOPVLVSQVEROMANVS
IMP·CAESARI·DIVI·NERVAE·F·NERVAE
TRAIANO·AVGGERM·DACICOPONTIF
MAXIMOTRIBPOT·XVIIIMPVICOSVIPP
ADDECLARANDVMQVANTAEALTITVDINIS
MONSETLOCVSTAN͞͞͞͞IBVSSITEGESTVS

Trajan's column is the most famous example of Roman capitalis.

Book producers at work in a monastic scriptorium thought to be the Abbey of Echternach. © UNIVERSITÄTSBIBLIOTHEK BREMEN, MS 217, C. 1020

Carolingian minuscule script from the Freising manuscripts, the oldest documents in Slovene and the first Slavic texts to be written in Latin script.

German polyhistor, theologian, and divine Johannes Trithemius (1462–1516), c. 1505. HULTON ARCHIVE/GETTY IMAGES

Portrait of Erasmus of Rotterdam by Quentin Massys, 1517. GALLERIA NAZIONALE D'ARTE ANTICA

Incipit liber bresith quem nos genesim dicimus. In principio creauit deus celum et terram. Terra autem erat inanis et vacua: et tenebre erant super faciem abissi: et spiritus domini ferebatur super aquas. Dixitque deus. Fiat lux. Et facta est lux. Et vidit deus lucem quod esset bona: et diuisit lucem a tenebris: appellauitque lucem diem et tenebras noctem. Factumque est vespere et mane dies vnus. Dixit quoque deus. Fiat firmamentum in medio aquarum: et diuidat aquas ab aquis. Et fecit deus firmamentum: diuisitque aquas que erant sub firmamento ab hijs que erant super firmamentum: et factum est ita. Vocauitque deus firmamentum celum: et factum est vespere et mane dies secundus. Dixit vero deus. Congregentur aque que sub celo sunt in locum vnum: et appareat arida. Et factum est ita. Et vocauit deus aridam terram: congregationesque aquarum appellauit maria. Et vidit deus quod esset bonum: et ait. Germinet terra herbam virentem et facientem semen: et lignum pomiferum faciens fructum iuxta genus suum: cuius semen in semetipso sit super terram. Et factum est ita. Et protulit terra herbam virentem et facientem semen iuxta genus suum: lignumque faciens fructum et habens vnumquodque sementem secundum speciem suam. Et vidit deus quod esset bonum: et factum est vespere et mane dies tercius. Dixitque autem deus. Fiant luminaria in firmamento celi: et diuidant diem ac noctem: et sint in signa et tempora et dies et annos: vt luceant in firmamento celi et illuminent terram. Et factum est ita. Fecitque deus duo luminaria magna: luminare maius vt preesset diei et luminare minus vt preesset nocti et stellas: et posuit eas in firmamento celi vt lucerent super terram: et

preessent diei ac nocti: et diuiderent lucem ac tenebras. Et vidit deus quod esset bonum: et factum est vespere et mane dies quartus. Dixit eciam deus. Producant aque reptile anime viuentis et volatile super terram sub firmamento celi. Creauitque deus cete grandia: et omnem animam viuentem atque motabilem quam produxerant aque in species suas: et omne volatile secundum genus suum. Et vidit deus quod esset bonum: benedixitque eis dicens. Crescite et multiplicamini: et replete aquas maris: auesque multiplicentur super terram. Et factum est vespere et mane dies quintus. Dixit quoque deus. Producat terra animam viuentem in genere suo: iumenta et reptilia et bestias terre secundum species suas. Factumque est ita. Et fecit deus bestias terre iuxta species suas: et iumenta et omne reptile terre in genere suo. Et vidit deus quod esset bonum: et ait. Faciamus hominem ad ymaginem et similitudinem nostram: et presit piscibus maris: et volatilibus celi et bestijs vniuerseque terre: omnique reptili quod mouetur in terra. Et creauit deus hominem ad ymaginem et similitudinem suam: ad ymaginem dei creauit illum: masculum et feminam creauit eos. Benedixitque illis deus: et ait. Crescite et multiplicamini: et replete terram: et subicite eam: et dominamini piscibus maris: et volatilibus celi: et vniuersis animantibus que mouentur super terram. Dixitque deus. Ecce dedi vobis omnem herbam afferentem semen super terram: et vniuersa ligna que habent in semetipsis sementem generis sui: vt sint vobis in escam et cunctis animantibus terre: omnique volucri celi et vniuersis que mouentur in terra: et in quibus est anima viuens: vt habeant ad vescendum. Et factum est ita. Viditque deus cuncta que fecerat: et erant valde bona.

Page from the Gutenberg Bible.

SPECIAL STUDIES OF THE CAPITALS, SMALL LETTERS, AND FIGURES

A B C D E F G H I J K L M
N O P Q R S T U V W X Y Z

a b c d e f g h i j k l m n o p
q r s t u v w x y z 1 2 3 4 5 6 7 8 9 0.

Pupils who have studied and followed the explanations, suggestions, and instructions so far, will have sufficient control of the muscular movement to master easily the letters on this page.

Those who have not been thorough in studying the instruction and practicing the drills should review. Nothing less than failure can follow superficial study.

The capitals, small letters, and figures are given at this point for convenient reference, and an effort should be made hereafter to employ these forms in all the written work.

One lesson each week should be devoted to special study and practice of the capitals until they are mastered.

Capitals, small letters, and figures will all be taught thoroughly in the following lessons.

A few minutes in the right way are worth more than hours of practice in the wrong way.

Page from *The Palmer Method of Business Writing.*
Cedar Rapids: A. N. Palmer Co., 1915. INTERNET ARCHIVE

The Spencerian alphabet.

Portrait of Platt Rogers Spencer.
The Spencerian Key to Practical Penmanship by H. C. Spencer, 1866.
THE UNIVERSITY OF SOUTH CAROLINA
RARE BOOKS & SPECIAL COLLECTIONS

Movement Exercises.

Spencer's method broke down letters into common elements based on natural forms. After his death in 1864, his family continued to dominate American penmanship instruction, marketing books like *The Spencerian Key to Practical Penmanship* to schools across the country. THE UNIVERSITY OF SOUTH CAROLINA RARE BOOKS & SPECIAL COLLECTIONS

Early Sholes and
Glidden typewriter.
PHOTOQUEST/
GETTY IMAGES

Portrait of Mark Twain
by Abdullah Frères, 1867.
COURTESY OF THE
LIBRARY OF CONGRESS

Chapter 8

A DEVILISH CONTRIVANCE

O NE OF THE "quill drivers" or "pen pushers" from the nineteenth century was the title character of Herman Melville's famous short story "Bartleby, the Scrivener: A Story of Wall Street." Hired by a lawyer to copy legal documents as the third scrivener in a firm, he laboriously works his pen while holed up in his office day after day. He and his colleagues are latter-day monks in an industrial-era scriptorium. After an initial spurt of energetic copying, Bartleby stops doing any writing. Then he stops doing anything at all. He responds to every request, either passive-aggressively or in the spirit of civil disobedience, with the phrase "I prefer not to." Eventually, Bartleby prefers not to write, move, or, eventually, eat. It is rumored, at the end of the story, that Bartleby's job after the legal office was in that most moribund of places for the handwriter: the Dead Letter Office.

As with the Spencerian and Palmer Method manuals that instructed students to do handwriting drills for six to twelve hours a day, Melville's story about the repetitive, dulling actions of the scribe's work reveals both the importance and drudgery of pen and paper in mid-nineteenth-century America. Even after a boy finished school and went to work, if handwriting was part of his job description, it was anything but creative or expressive. Not only was the work unending, but it could not be hurried. Handwriting was—and is—slow. The year Melville's story was published, 1853, the handwriting speed record was 30 words a minute.*[1]

Not surprisingly, many people in America and elsewhere were tinkering with prototypes of a "writing machine" that would allow letters to be stamped quickly, instead of being slowly formed using loops and curves. It would also allow letters, documents, and manuscripts to be read more quickly as well, because the writing would be uniform and more accommodating to the eye. By the 1860s several such machines had been invented; however, none of these proto-typewriters sped up the pace of writing. The first people to use "type-writers," as they

---

* To illustrate this speed, going at the rate of 30 words per minute— *the very fastest anyone could write*—you would not finish copying the first sentence of this paragraph in one minute. The *average* pace was even slower.

were immediately called, went slower than 30 words per minute when they typed. Nor were typewriters economical: the early models cost about $100, whereas pens went for about a dime.[2]

One inventor, Christopher Lapham Sholes, eventually developed a model for a writing machine with more potential, and sold it to E. Remington & Sons. In post–Civil War America, the demand for Eliphalet Remington's legendary rifles was waning, so he decided to beat guns into typewriters. He and co-inventor Carlos Glidden marketed the new product, a heavy, loud metal machine mounted on a table with a treadle at the bottom, as the Sholes & Glidden "Type Writer." It cost $125 and looked like a jury-rigged sewing machine.

It was no viral sensation. Not only was it costly, but it was also heavy, cumbersome, and noisy. In Jack London's novel *John Barleycorn*, the protagonist has one of the early models and reports that "it sounded like distant thunder of someone breaking up the furniture . . . I had to hit the keys so hard that I strained my first fingers to the elbows, while the ends of my fingers were blisters burst and blistered again." The only way you could see the letters you had written was by lifting the carriage up and peering inside.

Authors were early adopters of the typewriter. This was partially calculated. In the 1870s and 1880s, typewriter manufacturers marketed the machines primarily to novelists and clergymen, thinking they were the most likely to use them, as they generally wrote the most (in terms of volume of words) at the time. When the first Remingtons went on the market, only four hundred of the initial one thousand produced were sold. One of those four hundred was bought by a man always eager to get the latest gadget: Mark Twain. He saw his first typewriter in a shop window in 1874 and asked to see how it worked. As he remembered years later:

> The salesman explained it to us, showed us samples of its work, and said it could do fifty-seven words a minute—a statement which we frankly confessed that we did not believe. So he put his type-girl to work, and we timed her by the watch. She actually did the fifty-seven in sixty seconds. We were partly convinced, but said it probably couldn't happen again. But it did. We timed the girl over and over again—with the same result always: she won out. She did her work on narrow slips of paper, and we pocketed them as fast as she turned them out, to show as curiosities . . . I bought one, and we went away very much excited.
>
> At the hotel we got out our slips and were a little disappointed to find that they contained the same words. The girl had economized time and labor by using a formula which she knew by heart. However, I argued—safely enough—that the FIRST type-girl

must naturally take rank with the first billiard-player: neither of them could be expected to get out of the game any more than a third or a half of what was in it. If the machine survived—IF it survived—experts would come to the front, by and by, who would double the girl's output without a doubt. They would do one hundred words a minute—my talking speed on the platform.[3]

Twain went home and "played with the toy, repeating and repeating and repeating 'The Boy Stood on the Burning Deck' until I could turn that boy's adventure out at the rate of 12 words a minute." But he used it only for show. After Twain was done playing, he "reverted to pen and paper for all other writing." He kept the typewriter, but "only worked the machine to astonish visitors."

Twain eventually determined what would be true for male professionals in the next century: the best way to use a typewriter was to hire a female type-writer to take dictation. Twain "hired a young woman, and did my first dictating (letters, merely) . . . The machine did not do both capitals and lower case . . . but only capitals. Gothic capitals they were, and sufficiently ugly."[4]

A boy wrote Twain a letter, hoping for a specimen of Twain's handwriting and an autograph. Twain decided to foil him by sending him a machine-made response: "I furnished it—in type-machine capitals, signature and all.

It was long; it was a sermon; it contained advice; also reproaches. I said writing was my trade, my bread and butter: I said it was not fair to ask a man to give away samples of his trade; would he ask the blacksmith for a horseshoe? Would he ask the doctor for a corpse?"

Twain would subsequently brag in his autobiography that he was "the first person in the world to apply the type-machine to literature." He did not actually bang out the words but rather dictated parts of *The Adventures of Tom Sawyer*. As he wrote, a "young woman . . . copied a considerable part of a book of mine."[5] "Dictating autobiography to a typewriter is a new experience for me, but it goes very well, and is going to save time and 'language'—the kind of language that soothes vexation," he wrote.

Even with his hired help and the ability to have his words recorded for him, Twain soon tired of the awkward pedals, capital letters, and blind typing afforded by the first Remington model. When the company asked him to shill for the product, Twain refused.

Twain described the machine in 1905, remembering his first experiences with it decades earlier, as "full of caprices, full of defects—devilish ones. It had as many immoralities as the machine of today has virtues. After a year or two I found that it was degrading my character, so I thought I would give it to [William Dean] Howells [the novelist and editor of the *Atlantic Monthly*]. He was reluctant, for he was suspicious of novelties and unfriendly toward them, and he remains so to this day. But I persuaded him. He had great confidence in me, and I got him to believe things about the machine that I did not believe myself. He took it home to Boston, and my morals began to improve, but his have never recovered."

Gradually, the machine improved. In 1896, Remington added a carriage return, a convenient feature, and in 1898, Underwood rolled out a new model whose keys struck the top of the page so the letters could be seen as they were made. Sales started to pick up as typewriters became more user-friendly. By 1905, when Twain first published those memories of his adventures with the typewriter, Remington again asked him for a product endorsement. This time he said yes. In *Harper's* magazine Remington ran an ad featuring a picture of the 1875 model Twain made fun of, alongside Twain's snarky review. Below it was a picture of the 1905 model accompanied by a more recent endorsement:

I have dictated to a typewriter before. Between that experience and the present one there lies a mighty gap—more than thirty years! It is sort of a lifetime. In that wide interval much has happened—to the type-machine as well as to the rest of us. At the beginning of that interval a type-machine was a curiosity. The person who owned one was a curiosity, too. But now it is the other way about: the person who DOESN'T own one is a curiosity.

Twain was not the only novelist who was an early adopter of the typewriter. Henry James acquired the typewriter in the 1880s and became addicted to it: "He . . . reached a state at which the click of a Remington machine acted as a positive spur . . . During a fortnight when the Remington was out of order he dictated to an Olivetti typewriter with evident discomfort, and he found it almost disconcerting to speak to something that made no responsive sound at all."[6]

By the 1890s, James began dictating all his novels to a secretary, who typed the author's words as he said them aloud. At first James found it hard to find such an amanuensis who would understand his words. As he put it, "The young typists are mainly barbarians, and the civilized here are not typists," he declared, noting that hiring a woman was "an economy" over his previously male secretary.[7]

Dictating to a female type-writer alleviated the problem of James's poor handwriting. As he wrote in a letter to George Bernard Shaw:

I have been rather sharply unwell and obliged to stay my hand, for some days, from the pen. I am, thank goodness, better, but still not penworthy—and in fact feel as if I should never be so again in the presence of the beautiful and hopeless example your inscribed page sets me. Still another form of your infinite variety, this exquisite application of your ink to your paper! It is indeed humiliating. But I bear up, or try to—and the more that I can dictate, at least when I absolutely must.[8]

Some claim that the difference between James's "early" and "middle" styles stems from this move to dictation in the 1890s enabled by the typewriter. By 1907 he was doing it for all his work. As his secretary later remembered, once he started dictating, "its effects [became] easily recognisable in his style, which became more and more free, involved, unanswered talk . . . It all seems, he once explained, 'to be much more effectively and unceasingly *pulled* out of me in speech than in writing.'"*[9] Typewriter manufacturers began marketing their machines as alleviating some of the physical ills that ensue from the hours of handwriting that people like Bartleby, whose job involved creating documents, had to endure. The typewriter was

---

* Contemporary author Richard Powers is a latter-day James in this regard. He has used voice recognition software for years and defends the practice as aiding his creativity: "Writing is the act of accepting the huge shortfall between the story in the mind and what hits the page . . . For that, no interface will ever be clean or invisible enough for us to get the passage right." As Socrates knew, writing can never be unmediated in the way speech is. It always requires a technology.

advertised as a faster way to get work done that would also "guard against pen paralysis, loss of sight, and curvature of the spine."

This pitch initially failed to win over many businesses, because even if it was better for worker health, typewritten correspondence was deemed insulting and unprofessional. Nor did private individuals respond to the machine, as most assumed a typewritten personal letter had been dictated to a third party, and this was perceived as an invasion of privacy. Others felt receiving a typewritten letter indirectly implied the writer thought they were too uneducated to read longhand.[10]

In Jack London's 1909 fictionalized autobiography *Martin Eden*, the eponymous hero is a self-made writer who sends handwritten manuscripts of his short stories to magazine editors. Most are unceremoniously sent back to him, the rejections all typewritten. Frustrated by being turned down everywhere, Martin reads in a newspaper that "manuscripts should always be typewritten," rents a typewriter, spends a day learning how to use it, and begins to type up the handwritten stories. Some are accepted. Martin realizes only typewritten manuscripts will be taken seriously by literary editors, but he is often broke, and typewriters are expensive. He starts a cycle wherein he buys a typewriter, then hawks it when he needs money for food, and then buys it back again after he makes a sale.

To Martin, however, typewritten correspondence is off-putting because it is overly mechanical. He imagines editors as "cogs in a machine," echoing Bartleby's discomfort with being a slave to the quill. And Martin's writing becomes more mechanical as well when he follows the advice of writers' magazines to produce "machine-made storyettes." London's novel shows the transition from typewriters as a novelty to typewriters as the primary technology for writing.

To ease that transition, some companies offered "bridge" technologies not unlike what Apple, with its many print-based features, such as "copy and paste," did for early adopters of personal computers. For instance, one company offered an automatic form-letter typing machine that would produce a document indistinguishable from a handwritten letter. Another marketed—unsuccessfully, it appears—a typewriter whose letter keys were formed from handwriting of the buyer.

Eventually, most reservations were overcome, and typewriting became acceptable for business and personal correspondence. By 1910, two million typewriters had been sold.[11]

Although one would expect outcries against the typewriter from penmanship proponents, the early response from educators to the typewriter was largely positive. It helped with spelling and punctuation, teachers claimed:

"Teachers had noticed, early in the game, that the clarity of machine writing forced people to improve their spelling and punctuation. The penman, in doubt about whether the 'i' should proceed the 'e,' had usually written an ambiguous 'ie' that could be taken for 'ei.' Or had made the entire word a snakelike ripple that could be understood only from context." Others believed the typewriter helped children learn to read early: Entranced by the machine, they would start playing with it and, by default, learn their letters.[12] Researchers found that "familiarity with the typewriter makes students better penmen, not worse. The typewritten word seems to set a standard for neatness."[13]

That enthusiasm aside, after typing had become common, some groups began to lament the loss of proper penmanship instruction. "Since the introduction of the typewriter in our junior high schools, there is a tendency to minimize the importance of the teaching of handwriting," wrote a Pittsburgh school administrator in 1924.[14] In 1938 the *New York Times* published an article, "Of Lead Pencils," that warned, "Writing with one's own hand seems to be disappearing, and the universal typewriter may swallow all."[15]

The placement of the keys on the typewriter greatly influenced the speed of the typist. The letters were arranged into an idiosyncratic pattern—that, despite it being inefficient and of no purpose to us today, remains: the

QWERTY keyboard. QWERTY was invented in 1873 in order to separate common letter pairs, preventing type bars from sticking together when struck sequentially. But QWERTY keyboards did not come with any instruction manual for how best to use them. Most people used either two or four fingers to type.

In 1888, Frank McGurrin created a system that all people could use, one that would be the most efficient. His system is what we now call touch-typing. He went on the road, showing off his speedy new method, shocking people that he could hit keys without looking at them and using all ten fingers.

McGurrin challenged anyone to beat his speed. Louis Traub, a typewriting teacher in Cincinnati, took the bet. Traub was dismissive of the ten-finger system, asserting that four were enough. McGurrin and Traub dueled in Cincinnati in 1888, racing to see who could more quickly and accurately complete forty-five minutes of direct dictation and forty-five minutes of copying from an unfamiliar script. McGurrin, with his ten fingers and the "home keys" method of placement, won decisively.

The media and public were fascinated by the spectacle of typing contests. Going fast was becoming a cultural phenomenon in an increasingly industrialized America, and typing speed contests fit perfectly into this general speedup. Over the next few decades, typing races were a craze, and highly competitive.

Charles E. Smith had developed the Underwood Speed Training Group on Vesey Street in New York City. There, dozens of typists practiced eight hours a day. They had custom-fit racing typewriters: souped-up machines built for speed that they took to matches, exhibitions, and the world championships. Inside the warehouse on Vesey Street the training was intense, with each typist aware of how fast fellow competitors were going by the sound of the keys clicking.

Smith constantly tinkered with his system, introducing a new technique, the speed paper insert, that would take a second off a typist's time for each page; the typist had to take out a completed page and insert a new one while simultaneously moving the carriage return to the right.

Competitions were tense, with rows of people sitting at their machines. When the race started, the sounds of the machines typing about 140 words a minute was cacophonous. Each mistake penalized the competitor 10 words on his average. Mistakes included "writing more than seventy-six or less than sixty-one letters in a line," "if a letter failed to strike exactly in the middle of its space, or if the margin was not perfectly even, or if the escapement jumped a space."[16] Hitting the wrong letter, missing words, or misspelling were also mistakes.

Smith recruited a secretarial student, Stella Willins, who developed the capacity to type 264 words per minute when she was able to memorize in advance and type for one minute only.[17] At the peak of the "sport" of touch-typing, Willins won the world championships in 1926.

Being a fast typist—like having good handwriting in the early days of the Renaissance—was a pathway to social mobility. One of the champion speed typists, Cortez Peters (141 words per minute of unfamiliar script), would go on to found one of the first black-owned business school franchises. Eventually, touch-typing made it into the educational curriculum and was taught in newly established high school courses in typewriting.

Only once typing became the de facto method to conduct business correspondence and keep records did handwriting assume the associations we have with it today: a way to express one's uniqueness and personality. It is only in the twentieth century that handwriting becomes evidence of—and a way to analyze—the individual psyche.

Chapter 9

LONG DESCENDERS

Many theories over centuries have linked character to physical traits. One's face is said to show character; the eyes are the window of the soul or, as it says in the book of Isaiah, "the show of their countenance doth witness against them." The Greeks sometimes judged people according to which animal they supposedly looked like: those with "dog-like" noses were short-tempered, while those with "lion-like" noses were generous.[1] Even handwriting was occasionally used to mark temperament before the nineteenth century: the emperor Nero apparently said of one of his courtiers that "his handwriting showed him treacherous,"[2] and an eleventh-century Chinese philosopher stated that "handwriting can infallibly show whether it comes from a person who is noble-minded, or from one who is vulgar."[3]

One of the first to argue that handwriting was related to personal character was a seventeenth-century Italian doctor, Camillo Baldi, who developed a theory and wrote a pamphlet explaining his system. "If the writing is both fast, even and well-formed, and appears to have been written with pleasure, it has probably been written by a man who knows nothing and is worthless, because you rarely find intelligent and prudent men who write neatly"[4]; however, "if the handwriting is uneven . . . he is likely to be choleric and apt to be unrestrained in following his desires." No one took to Baldi's system, probably because they could not conceptualize such a link, as handwriting at the time was more often correlated with status and rank, not individuality. A few other Europeans followed in Baldi's wake, but their attempts to sell their insights into human character failed as well, save some traveling minstrels who performed handwriting analysis in circuses and as party tricks.

The conception that handwriting might offer insight into the writer began to gain traction in the late eighteenth- and early nineteenth-century Romantic era, when spontaneity, originality, and individuality were prized. In America, such a Romantic interest in handwriting took the form of autograph collecting and analysis of the signatures of famous people. Edgar Allan Poe helped popularize this trend in a series he wrote for *Graham's* magazine that aimed "to give the Autograph signature—that is, a facsimile in woodcut—of each of our most distinguished literati; second, to maintain that the character is, to a certain extent, indicated by the chirography; and thirdly, to embody, under each Autograph signature—some literary gossip about the individual, with a brief critical comment on his writings."[5] Poe's critiques revealed as much about his own literary tastes and prejudices as anything else. He wrote that William Cullen Bryant, whose writing Poe did not like, had handwriting that looked like "one of the most commonplace clerk's hands which we ever encountered, and has no character about it beyond that of the day-book and ledger." A now-obscure female author showed "a strong disposition to fly off at a tangent."[6] Poe felt those who wrote as they had been instructed were less original than those whose handwriting departed from what they were taught in school.

By the mid-nineteenth century, a new hobby, auto-graph collecting, became popular, and autograph albums proliferated. Collectors asked illustrious figures to provide samples of their signatures, sometimes by writing to them and sometimes by asking them in person. But the most treasured signatures were those done without premedita-tion, garnered from the famous person unawares. As one collector advised: "We should come by it obliquely, and not by direct attack. A name written at the request of a stranger is only about as valuable as the same name stamped by machinery. To have any character, it should have been written in a careless or confidential moment."[7] Therefore, so-called autograph harpies, as they were called, would come up with excuses—for example, asking a congressman to sign a fake petition.

Collectors ascribed a certain magic to these autographs. Through gaining a sample of a famous person's writing, they could "drink inspiration from original fountains." The well-known being solicited often got annoyed. One commented that it was like being asked for "a lock of one's mental and moral hair," and another that it was "a subtraction from our potency."[8]

It is a short step from prizing autographs by authors to believing handwriting reveals the inner self of ordinary folk, too, and to wondering if the strict lessons of writing masters were perhaps suffocating people's individuality. Isaac D'Israeli, a British essayist (and father of Benjamin Disraeli), was another early handwriting romantic, and worried in 1823 that rote schooling was making people too mechanical; he thought writing masters made script too standardized and uniform. "Regulated as the pen is now too often by a mechanical process . . . the true physiognomy of writing will be lost among our rising generation."[9] He argued that British writing masters forced students to use "automatic motions, as if acted on by the pressure of a steam-engine," a method which ultimately produced writing "all appearing to have come from the same rolling-press . . . Our hand-writings [are as] monotonous as our characters in the present habits of society."[10] D'Israeli's critiques spoke to the nation that handwriting was something distinguishable from what is machine-made, something that connotes individuality.

Graphology as a formal enterprise and a theory was invented when a French clergyman, Abbé Jean-Hippolyte Michon, yoked empirical science to the idea one could deduce character from handwriting. Born in 1806 in a village in western France, he was ordained as a priest in 1830. He served in a small parish school until 1842, when the church was closed. One of the other teachers at the school, Father Flandrin, a philosophy professor, told him about the analysis of character through handwriting. After the school closed, Michon took to preaching around France. He wrote treatises on the archaeology and history of his area of the country and was asked to travel to the Holy Land with a group of archaeologists, the only priest among scientists. He became one the best-known liberal Catholics of the time, founding a magazine in Paris calling for greater separation between church and state, reduced papal power, and greater democracy among the clergy. He published a book, *On the Renewal of the Church*, in 1860, which the Church promptly put in the *Index of Prohibited Books*. He was forced to publicly retract the book, after which he turned to writing pseudonymous anticlerical novels, including *The Maudit*, about a young priest struggling to reconcile his liberal views with the Church establishment. (*The Maudit* was a hit, translated into many languages, and although the Church tried to ferret out the author unsuccessfully, only after Michon's death was his handiwork revealed.)[11]

After the first Vatican Council in 1868, which strengthened the power of the then ultraconservative church under Pope Pius IX, Michon became even more disillusioned and stopped fighting for reform. He started preaching for a new cause: handwriting analysis.

Michon's first book on handwriting was *The Mysteries of Handwriting*, published in 1872 with Adolphe Desbarrolles, who believed in the relationship between handwriting and the occult. Michon quickly disavowed that book, given its association with the occult, as well as Desbarrolles's work, which he did not think was sufficiently scientific. He founded a journal, *La Graphologie: Journal de l'autographes*, which, in its inaugural issue on November 18, 1871, used the term "graphology" for the first time. Michon offered free handwriting analysis to the journal's first subscribers. He followed that with a lecture announcing his new science and then traveled across France and Europe to explain and demonstrate graphology. Michon evangelized for his cause: "Graphology has proved itself to be a new tool for the moral world . . . one that has appeared through divine intervention at the height of material advances brought about by the discovery of the steam engine and electricity."[12]

Michon published two further books elucidating his system, *La méthode pratique de graphologie* and *Système de graphologie*. A third text, *Histoire de Napoléon ler d'après son écriture*, was devoted to analyzing Napoleon's handwriting throughout his life. In these books, Michon drilled into readers the importance of practicing graphology scientifically, which meant conducting painstakingly detailed empirical research. "I began by classifying my collection of autographs of strong-willed authors and weak-willed authors," Michon wrote of his rigorous scientific method. "The comparative research of thousands of handwriting samples shows that all weak-willed people cross their 't's feebly. The line is always weak, filiform, and terminates with a scarcely noticeable pin-head . . . [I]n contrast, all strong-willed writers cross their 't's forcefully and firmly, while exerting strong pressure on their pens."[13]

Michon worked to link religion and science to present a theory that would undergird both: that the soul shows itself scientifically through handwriting. Michon felt this did not occur in handwriting taught in school but rather when someone "enters into spontaneous and free life and wants to express his thoughts and feelings towards other people quickly, without effort, without study, without being concerned in the least about forming letters well or badly." Then "he instinctively abandons his habits of calligraphy and shifts to a writing with unique characteristics":

This philosophy of the manifestation of the soul through graphic signs is based on the intimate connection which exists between each sign . . . which emanates from the human personality, and the soul, which is the substance of that personality. Who can doubt that every word is the spontaneous and immediate translation of thought? And who can doubt that handwriting is as spontaneous and immediate a translation of thought as speech? All handwriting, like all language, is the immediate manifestation of the intimate, intellectual and moral being.[14]

Michon's ideas caught on in Germany later in the nineteenth century. In 1890s Germany, the main proponent of graphology was Wilhelm Preyer, a physiologist who stated that handwriting was "brain writing." Preyer divided the brain into the "mind," which is rational (ego), and the "soul," over which we have less control (id), and argued mind and soul are revealed through the motor actions one takes when writing. Preyer's disciple, Ludwig Klages, explained that, in handwriting, the movement between mind and soul is "caught" and can be interpreted. A clerk writing a letter for his supervisor, Klages argued, would use standard-size letters, since he is at work; but when he writes a letter to his beloved, his true nature would come out, whether through larger capitals, wider spaces between words, or any of the many identifying signs of graphology.[15]

As the Germans took on graphology, Michon's concept of the soul was slowly replaced by Freudian and Jungian theories of instinctual drives and psychological complexes to explain what comes out of our pens. The German psychoanalyst graphologists added more identifying signs; if someone put a lot of pressure on the pen, for instance, he had a strong libido. If he used "downward plunging strokes," he had an earthy nature. As Freudian and Jungian theories of the individual psyche spread, so would the psychological analysis of handwriting. Other European countries developed graphological societies, and the science crossed to America in the twentieth century when June Downey published *Graphology and the Psychology of Handwriting* in 1919.

As graphology spread, it joined other pseudosciences, such as phrenology and eugenics, that used fake empiricism to discriminate. Phrenologists claimed that measuring the size of skulls and areas of the brain could determine character. Phrenology was used to justify European superiority over other races—even to create a hierarchy of races based on skull shapes—and to claim male superiority over women. Eugenics examined hereditary traits to make similar false claims about the superiority of races, ethnicities, and genders and advocated reproducing desired heredity traits and eliminating undesirable ones. Graphology had a role in similarly unsavory practices: Thomas Byerley, a British journalist, argued the physical act of writing could not be faked and so could be used to determine criminality and mental illness, unlike "in all other actions . . . [in which] some share of guile and deception may lurk, which it requires penetration, experience, and skill to be able to detect."[16] Byerley claimed handwriting tells all. Exceptions were made to so-called rules of graphology to help smooth out problematic conclusions. For instance, geniuses with bad handwriting were excused from being labeled idiots, aberrants, or criminals because "men of intellect sometimes work under great nervous tension. They see ahead and feel the spirit of that which they are writing, and thoughts flow too quickly for the pen."[17] The flourishes and ascenders of a person's script became a common tool for assessing employees to ascertain, for instance, if applicants are controlled by their minds, "indicated by the smoothness, evenness and refinement of their pen strokes; others are controlled by their bodily appetites, as indicated by the thickness and coarseness of the strokes," wrote one expert.[18] Graphologists had a steady business counseling people before answering marriage proposals as well.

Graphology continued to be popular, if slightly less so, throughout the increasingly empirical twentieth century. Today it is practiced by licensed experts, and in some cases handwriting by job applicants is analyzed by a graphologist as a precondition for employment. The British Academy of Graphology, founded in 1985, offers a diploma upon completion of a three-year course at the London College of Graphology. Continental Europeans, who invented graphology, are still the most serious about it. The European Deontological Association of Graphologists was founded in 1900 to "unite the European Graphological Associations in applying graphology on a higher scientific and quality level." They adhere to the "Code of Deontology," which outlines fourteen principles, including never displaying one's graphological qualifications on professional documents "if these are associated with an activity concerned with the occult or divination" and abstaining from "issuing diagnoses in fields reserved for the medical profession."[19] The association comprises groups from western European countries: Switzerland, Germany, Italy, Spain, Belgium, the Netherlands, and France.

The French are the most active practitioners of graphology. Graphologists claim that more than half of employers use graphology to some extent when screening job candidates (although the real number is hard to verify, as many employers do not disclose this practice, and some may use it only occasionally). Catharine Bottiau, a leading French graphologist, explains that "normally we are consulted once the client has already drawn up a shortlist of candidates. Then the candidates will be asked to write a motivational letter, using their own handwriting. We will examine the letters, and offer our advice. Usually this will tend to confirm the impressions already gleaned from interviews, the CV, personality tests and so on. But sometimes we can draw attention to aspects of personality that have been missed, and which might prove detrimental were the person to be recruited."[20] A headhunter in France acknowledges that it works but he has no idea why: "Look, I place 100 or so people every year in very senior international positions. If graphology didn't work, it would quickly become obvious, and I would lose my clients. But they keep coming back. I have no idea how it works, but to me it is obvious: the handwriting of a marketing guy is not the same as the handwriting of a sales guy, which is not the same as the handwriting of an artist or of an accountant!"[21]

Andrea McNichol's 1991 *Handwriting Analysis: Putting It to Work for You* offers strategies for individuals to analyze people in their life, such as "who is lying about his age, which potential mate is more considerate, who cheated his customer and which babysitter is on drugs." McNichol, whose author bio states that she has been "consulted by the FBI, the U.S. Department of Justice, Scotland Yard, the U.S. Department of Defense, and Fortune 500 companies," explains that people who do not dot their *i*'s are untidy, and those who write in all capital letters are egotistical. Stable people cross their *t*'s in the middle of the ascender (upward stroke). Those who slant their words to the right are forward looking, whereas those who slant to the left look backward. If you use long descenders, as in the bottom of the letter *g*, you are sad, and if there are excessively wide spaces between letters, you are abnormal. As McNichol explains: "Abnormally wide spacing is extremely strange and abnormal because so few people do this. Anytime you see a writing that is abnormal, it means that the writer in abnormal . . . The abnormal distance he puts between each letter symbolizes the abnormal distance he puts between himself and other people. So this person is socially isolated."[*22]

Whether or not one takes stock in the findings of graphology, its rise signaled the shift to the meaning of handwriting as the unconscious manifestation of the authentic inner self, a concept we continue to hold today. Each person's handwriting is considered unique. Why not, then, introduce handwriting as evidence in a court of law—to attempt to prove, say, that Grandpa really did change his will on his deathbed?

---

[*] Arthur Storey's 1922 guide, *A Manual of Graphology or the Study of Handwriting*, interprets wide spaces differently, stating they indicate "lavishness, generosity and lucidity."

Chapter 10

QUESTIONED DOCUMENTS

KATHERINE SCHOENBERGER IS a forensic document examiner: Her job is to determine whether a document is authentic or bogus and then to testify about her findings in courts of law. If an heir contests a will, Schoenberger can be called upon to determine whether its signature is genuine. If someone receives an anonymous note in the mail, she could be hired to assess who might have written it.

The range of documents that Schoenberger might be hired to forensically examine is broad—from scrawled notes on bathroom walls to marks on paper calendars and letters from angry members of a homeowners' association. Many are "death related"—contracts, wills, estates, and powers of attorney—that contain signatures whose authenticity is under dispute in a legal case.

Forensic document examiners, whose work is based on science and evidence as opposed to psychology, see themselves as far more expert and accurate than graphologists. Trained in police laboratories, they work with pen tips and paper watermarks instead of upward strokes, and are uninterested in deducing personality traits or psychoanalyzing people by their writing. They just want to find out who the writer was and then prove it in a court of law. But they are involved, broadly, in the same questions: Do we each have a unique script? Is handwriting like snowflakes or fingerprints, something that is never exactly duplicated?

Schoenberger's dream, as a kid, was to be Quincy, the forensic pathologist star of the 1980s television show. "Quincy was my role model! But then I started taking pre-med classes and realized I was more interested in things than in bodies. I just wanted to explore and investigate." She went to Michigan State for an M.A. degree in forensic science, then spent two years being exhaustively trained in a Mississippi crime lab.

The variety of ways one can forge a signature—and, by definition, authenticate one—are dizzying. Schoenberger had to learn about different types of paper, pen, and inks, how to deal with burnt documents, torn paper, and photocopies made by laser printers, ink-jet printers, typewriters, fax machines, and photocopiers. Schoenberger can take a grid, lay it over a document, and check to see if it has been run through a printer or photocopier twice; she can tell if something written in ink on a printed piece of paper was added before or after it was run through the printer. She had to learn how to identify indentations on a piece of paper; using a pencil to shade over words that may be hidden is now bad form, and she uses an electronic static data apparatus to reveal the secret words on an apparently blank sheet.

Although she had to learn the Palmer Method, D'Nealian, Zaner-Bloser, and other American scripts, few of her cases require her to testify about them. More commonly she finds corroborating evidence through pens (ballpoint pens have wear on the metal tips that can indicate if the pen was used clockwise or counterclockwise), paper, or indentations. Writing tools such as pens and toner are more reliably unique than any one person's handwriting.

To authenticate a document, Schoenberger needs a "known sample," ideally several. She solved one case by identifying the font used on the printed envelope of a letter. "It was an unfamiliar type style. I searched fonts, and I identified it as Eva Antiqua. That font is not included in the standard fonts used by Word. I paid to buy the font and put it on my computer to test it. If the suspect had Eva Antiqua on her computer, that would help corroborate the case against her."

However, this sort of corroboration—a series of matches that indicate probability—is about as close to "certain" that Schoenberger can get. Her own judgment has changed as she gains more experience: "I have become less and less sure if a document is authentic or bogus as I get older. I know less as I learn more."

Lawyers have had a difficult time introducing hand-writing as evidence since the practice began in England, in 1836, when a judge, John Taylor Coleridge (the poet Samuel Taylor Coleridge's nephew), admitted it in his landmark case, *Doe v. Suckermore*. Coleridge's ruling was restrictive: A letter or signature could be introduced as evidence only if someone who knew the writer witnessed the act of writing—testimony in which the eyewitness also had to know the character of the person. As Coleridge put it: "We best acquire a knowledge of [handwriting] character, by seeing the individual write at times when his manner of writing is not in question . . . in his natural manner."[1] If a grandmother once saw her grandson writing a letter, she could testify as an expert on his handwriting. Postmen, who arguably saw more of an individual's handwriting than anyone—or family members who had never seen a defendant write—were disqualified. Witnesses had to have a sense of the individual as a person, because handwriting and character had been linked in the eighteenth and nine-teenth centuries.[2]

By the late nineteenth century, changes in society and conceptions of handwriting created a need for new laws. More people were literate, meaning more handwriting could be introduced in cases; bureaucracy increased, creating more documents; empirical science was emergent, creating different expectations of witnesses; and handwriting was becoming less rigidly class based.

The premise that only someone who knew the character of a person and had witnessed the writer in action could testify in court caused judges in America to grumble that amateurs who had little familiarity with a case could decide it. One called handwriting "the most unsatisfactory species of evidence Courts of justice have to deal with."[3] In 1913, Congress passed the general comparison statute, which allowed "the introduction of admitted or proven handwriting exemplars for comparative purposes."[4] With this statute, handwriting became a legal way to identify an individual, and experts were required to testify on the veracity of that individual's handwriting received in evidence for the purposes of comparison.[5]

Master penmen quickly jumped into this newly formed specialty, rebranding themselves as handwriting experts with the title of "questioned document examiners." Daniel Ames was one of the first such examiners. Ames had authored penmanship copybooks through the 1890s,[6] but with the introduction of the typewriter and better pen technology, he and other itinerant men traveling the country giving penmanship lessons were finding it harder to drum up students. As penmen, they had used the same rhetoric as Spencer and Palmer: Their services would uplift citizens, making them more moral and Christian through penmanship. Now, as experts, they needed science, so they swapped religion for empiricism and, like graphologists, created a system.

A known sample was examined for "quality of line" (affected by pen position, pressure, rhythm, speed, tremor, skill, and other factors), form (including proportions, slant, beginning and ending strokes, flourishes, and the like), and spelling and punctuation (a consequence of education).[7] While this more scientifically rigorous method replaced the "disputatious metaphysics and the vague indications of subjective impressions" of testimony in the pre-statute era,[8] the correlation between detail—slant, pressure, proportions—and conclusion remained fuzzy. For instance, Ames analyzed loops, connections between letters, and letter forms to come to his conclusions in the courtroom. Underlying his claims was the idea that no one could possibly reproduce all these elements, thus they identified one unique individual. He stressed that by identifying numerous idiosyncrasies in a signature, he could be certain who wrote it, although he never specified a definitive number of idiosyncrasies that would count as "enough" proof.

Other "experts" used more dubious methods. Persifor Frazer used what he called "bibliotics," "grammapheny," and "plassopheny" to describe how he studied documents, handwriting, and forgery, respectively. He argued that if one could measure as many known samples as possible, one could then come up with averages (of degree of slant, height of ascenders, etc.) to come up with an "ideal" signature, a composite created from numerous photographs of that person's signed name, borrowing the method of Francis Galton, a major proponent of eugenics.

The search for the best way to identify the true, unconscious script of one unique person signaled a cultural shift in which handwriting came to be seen as the intimate expression of an individual and the signature as the symbol of the inner self's external manifestation. However, no expert could explain why his method of determining authenticity was sound, why some marks meant something significant when others did not, why slants were considered evidence, but how far into the right-hand margin a person wrote was not. The so-called experts underwent no training, although Ames claimed in defense of his own skills that just because a man is "an artist, an engraver, or a bank-teller, does not by any means make him an adept in discovering and explaining forgery."[9]

Not surprisingly, experts called on by competing parties came to differing conclusions, often insulting each other's methods and further diminishing their credibility in the eyes of the court.[10] Some judges refused to acknowledge the claims of handwriting experts in testimony. As one judge put it, comparing the science of handwriting identification to chemistry and biology: "What does the expert in handwriting profess to do? He has no scientific basis of education, experience, or laws to build on. As in this case, he simply compares one signature with others, and notes some differences, the causes of which he does not attempt to explain."[11] Outside the courtroom, handwriting experts were often seen as pretentious windbags and were pilloried in literary sketches such as the one that has a "Mr. Grapho" take off his glasses pretentiously before describing the "convolution of the G" and "perpendicularity of that I."

Despite this wobbly foundation, handwriting became the first example of forensics to be admissible in the courtroom, even though handwriting experts had authority *only* in the courtroom. Outside the courts, they had no authority. They were unlike doctors, or chemists, or other professionals with expert knowledge of their fields that could qualify them to testify in court. When handwriting experts were not testifying, they were merely teachers of italics or Spencerian, activities wholly unrelated to forensic science.

These new handwriting experts had a monopoly on their knowledge: The FBI, lacking any such professionals, would hire them. And as the science of handwriting analysis became more accepted, state crime labs started hiring questioned document specialists. By 1933 the FBI employed its own handwriting analysts in their technology laboratory.[12]

Thus, despite the lack of an absolute basis, handwriting

verification was assumed to rest on scientific knowledge: "The notion of expertise in handwriting identification was not only taken seriously but was viewed as beyond dispute, the kind of thing that reasonable people ought not even to question."[13]

Until 1993. In *Daubert v. Merrell Dow Pharmaceuticals*, the Supreme Court decided that judges must allow only scientific testimony whose "reasoning or methodology" was "scientifically valid."[14] Many forms of forensic evidence suddenly became potentially inadmissible—even fingerprinting. And handwriting analysis, always on shaky scientific grounds, became particularly dubious.

Katherine Schoenberger embarked on her career in forensic document examining only since the *Daubert* ruling, so her services have been in less demand than they would have been thirty years earlier. She does not agree with *Daubert*, because, she says, lawyers and judges lack the training she has. However, of the small group of licensed forensic document examiners, "it is getting us motivated to prove ourselves. It is not a subjective thing, handwriting examination." She admits that the field gets increasingly difficult to master as new technologies are introduced. In the early 1900s experts were looking at marks made by pens with nibbed tips, which had a lot of individual characteristics—more than ballpoint pens, invented in the 1940s. Schoenberger finds writing done with ballpoint pens easier to work with than writing done with fluid ink pens, introduced in the 1960s, because "fluid ink balls up and seeps into the page." Computer-generated documents offer other challenges.

However, according to Schoenberger, the courts are not the profession's biggest worry. The bigger problem comes from the ranks of the many "non-reputable people out there"—graphologists of various sorts—who pass themselves off as experts. "[Graphologists] learned a different theory and feel they can translate it but they didn't have the same training." Most graphologists who testify in court have degrees based on correspondence courses and are focused on what Schoenberger describes as who "people really are" rather than "whether documents a and b were written by the same person." Many lawyers do not understand the difference between graphologists and document examiners, so they hire people with graphological training to testify before judges who are similarly ignorant. Graphologists also generally charge less and can present impressive-sounding credentials, such as membership in an official-sounding group like the "National Handwriting Association."

What counted as testimony in the nineteenth century—an eyewitness to the act of writing—does not count today. What counted in 1920—an "expert" ascertaining whether two documents were written by the same person—does not hold water in the twenty-first century, when standards of scientific methodology are too high for side-by-side comparisons to overcome. Many legal experts argue that Schoenberger's methods are not scientifically valid, so if we agree with them and the ruling from *Daubert*, then it is impossible to prove one person's handwriting, which means handwriting does not express ineluctable individuality. Now, with the things we use to write—our ink and paper and the pages underneath on the pad—a person's handwriting can often be scientifically proven, and much of Schoenberger's cases rest on materials. But our slants and *t* bars would not be upheld in a court of law.

If handwriting's evidentiary status is in dispute, is it possible to even guess, let along prove, the authorship of computer-generated documents? In fact, computers can make deductions about the writer by considering word-processed files and e-mails, although the way they do it is not analogous to how handwriting experts evaluate handwritten evidence. Rather than noting how hard someone tends to press keys (corresponding to pressure on a page) or the pace of typing (corresponding to strokes), computers judge writing style: How the words are deployed and their algorithms can determine individuality better than handwriting experts can by analyzing linguistic patterns. The words you use leave a "thumbprint," or script, that may be more reliable than the way you make the downward stroke on a lowercase *y*.

The most famous case thus far in the emergent field of digital forensics is a low-stakes, fun example of sleuthing.

In 2013 a novel called *The Cuckoo's Calling* was published by Mulholland Books. Rumors flew that the novel was actually authored by J. K. Rowling. Could anyone prove she wrote it?

Patrick Juola, a computer scientist, ran the novel through a program that looked at patterns in word usage, common words, word length, and "character n-grams," or character pairs. He compared *The Cuckoo's Calling* with Rowling's previous novel, *The Casual Vacancy*, and concluded that those two books had more similarities to each other than *The Cuckoo's Calling* did with other books.

Another computer scientist, Peter Millican, ran further tests. Millican has developed the perfectly named software program, Signature, to analyze texts by finding patterns in word use as well as punctuation, sentence length, and paragraph length. He ran the Harry Potter series through Signature and got the same results Juola did: There were many similarities between the Harry Potter books and *The Cuckoo's Calling*. After the results were published, Rowling admitted authorship.[15]

Analyzing Rowling's writing style, a practice called stylometrics, at first blush seems "less scientific"—a bit mushy and soft, as it were—than analysis of materials and angles. But inasmuch as it concerns the actual expression of ideas instead of fine motor skills, stylometrics attends to the ideas and expressions in writing, a contextual approach. What words are often repeated? What is the writer's "voice"? What are her syntactical tics? Does she overly rely on the semicolon? A recent stylometric analysis of *Double Falsehood*, a disputed play by William Shakespeare, was proved to be partially the work of the Bard after it was run through computers, along with other known works by Shakespeare as well as those by Shakespeare contemporaries John Fletcher and Lewis Theobald—millions of words in all—to find patterns in sentence length, use of prepositions, unusual words, and other elements of each author's "fingerprint."

The new field of digital forensics recalls less the work of the CSI technician than the English professor. But over the past century people have developed more sophisticated forensic tools to authenticate documents only to achieve less conclusive results. Analyzing patterns of word use is not only potentially as reliable as analyzing pen strokes but arguably more interesting. Stylometrics promises to help us understand syntactical patterns, rhetorical habits, and other conceptual elements of writing.

English professors as well as librarians are also developing new ways to preserve and revive handwriting in a world in which most words are typed. Their efforts may result in a rise in the cultural and historical value of handwriting—and, as longhand drafts of novels become rarer, the financial value as well.

Chapter 11

DIGITAL HANDWRITING

O N T H E S I X T H floor of the stone and glass building that contains the Harry Ransom Humanities Center on the Austin campus of the University of Texas, between white boxes containing an original Maurice Ravel score and *Gone With the Wind* film stock, sit a few shelves of paperbacks. They are from the David Foster Wallace collection. The paperbacks include a copy of Don DeLillo's *White Noise*, its pages filled with the blue marker underlining and marginalia of the man now considered a twenty-first-century literary genius.

The Ransom Center, one of the most important research libraries in the country, with one of the largest collections of contemporary author archives in the world, is preserving all of Wallace's handwriting, along with thirty-six million other manuscripts pages, one million rare books, five million photographs, one hundred thousand works of art, and a Gutenberg Bible. But it is their post-1950 literary collection that they are most concerned with building today.[1]

Creating an archive of contemporary authors' papers presents challenges: Many authors, of course, have been word processing since the 1980s, and their manuscripts— that of Dreiser's *Sister Carrie*—are overwritten as they are revised, the first drafts lost to posterity. The authors included in the Ransom collection are those who have been wedded to handwriting. Although the center bought the platen Norman Mailer used to type *The Naked and the Dead*, it was no doubt the rest of Mailer's ten-ton, $2.5 million archive that prompted them to close the deal. "His mother saved everything!" said the guide looking at row after row of Mailer boxes filled with handwritten notes, letters, and drafts. The Ransom Center also has the longhand first drafts of novels by J. M. Coetzee, Ian McEwan, and Denis Johnson.

Thomas Staley, the longtime director, who retired in 2013, kept hunting for new talent: He had a photocopied list of some six hundred authors on whose careers he had an eye. He relied on influential friends, the staff reading group, and word on the street to give him tips. When Staley heard about an undergraduate reading Langston Hughes's poetry on campus one day, he asked the student which other poets he read, and noted down their names.

The center is wagering these authors will be the ones twenty-second-century Ph.D. students will pore over, whose novels will be released as "classic editions," and whose friendships with each other will become biography fodder. It is a gamble. What if authors in their collection drop off the literary map, their novels stocking the remainder tables? Staley is a realist: "Ten percent of an archive is worth 90 percent of its value, and 90 percent of an archive is worth 10 percent of the price."

The David Foster Wallace papers, along with the James Joyce and Samuel Beckett holdings, are now part of that 10 percent. Wallace in particular has spurred an uptick in off-the-street visits to the reading room. A woman walked in carrying a copy of Wallace's *Consider the Lobster and Other Essays* and asked how to apply for a research card. (All you need is a driver's license.) Fans trek across the country for the chance to see Wallace's handwritten annotations in paperbacks and his marginalia on his typed early drafts. Some ask for his handwriting to be sent via e-mail, and the staff has received several requests from tattoo artists for PDFs of Wallace's handwriting.

To preserve the value of its archive, the Ransom Center needs to keep finding authors who leave, as Staley put it, "the tracks of the imagination" with their pens, who write longhand, or annotate their books by writing in the margins. In a sense, this enormous, bustling center is an institution dependent upon scrawled-upon scraps of paper.

For libraries like the Ransom Center, handwriting is not becoming less important: It is rising in literary and financial value as it ceases to have much practical function. Libraries adding to their handwritten manuscript collections might be better prepared for the future than those busily replacing shelving with computers, because their holdings are singular. At the same time, the libraries installing technology are also preserving handwriting by using its more successful successor, the computer. Many librarians are going through their files and taking out the handwritten items in their archival boxes, scanning them to create digital copies, and then putting them up on their websites for all to see.

So over the last decades, and for the first time in the history of handwriting, unique, brittle documents are no longer kept under tight guard, their contents, if not the paper itself, accessible to those without the urgent desire to see in person those singular documents (and then, say, request a library card so they can see how David Foster Wallace annotated Don DeLillo's novels).

Using sophisticated digital tools that allow us to view one page of, say, an eleventh-century Spanish manuscript produced in a scriptorium, we can view medieval manuscripts even better, given computer resolutions and the ability to expand the size of the page, than if we were to view the original under museum glass. We are able to see more pages than we could in a museum as well: Rare books are usually statically opened to one page, whereas the best digital displays of them allow you to virtually turn pages.

In an age when technology allows us to search texts astonishingly quickly, handwritten documents that have never been transcribed or uploaded are left out. Another set of librarians and scholars has been working to solve this gap in access and knowledge by entering the texts of handwritten manuscripts, not just the images of them, into their databases.

To enter the entire text of an eleventh-century Spanish manuscript, for instance, requires people who can read the words on those pages written in various and often difficult-to-decipher scripts. It also requires many hours, so some libraries and universities have asked the public to help them out by transcribing handwriting from their couches at home. They are literally crowdsourcing handwriting.

The National Archives' pilot program, launched in 2011, was called "Transcription Pilot Project." More than three hundred documents were loaded onto the archives' website, including "letters to a civil war spy, various laws and acts, presidential records, suffrage petitions, indictments, and fugitive slave case files," and the public was invited to "help the National Archives make historical documents more accessible [and] help the next person discover and use that record." The documents, a small sample of those contained in the archive, were organized into three levels of difficulty—beginner, intermediate, and advanced—and they provided explanations and links to those who wanted to learn basic paleography.

However, the pilot program ended very quickly, because citizens rapidly and accurately transcribed all the documents as they were loaded; even the "advanced" documents were easy for some. The same thing happened when the New York Public Library launched its "What's on the Menu?" crowdsourced transcription program, in which menus from nineteenth- and early twentieth-century restaurants were scanned and uploaded in 2011. In just weeks, the public accurately transcribed all 9,000 menus the library had scanned. Since then, the library has digitized additional menus, and as of the end of 2015, more than 17,000 of the 45,000 in their collection had been transcribed by the public.[2]

A third project, Transcribe Bentham, is digitizing the Bentham Papers' archive of more than 70,000 items handwritten by Jeremy Bentham. (Bentham was an influential eighteenth- and nineteenth-century British thinker best known for his theory of utilitarianism, whose papers are of enormous historical and philosophical importance.) Since the program was launched in 2010 by University College London, volunteers have transcribed more than 10,000 manuscripts, or some 5.5 million words. Some of the documents are being read for the first time by these transcriptionists, and they are finding important nuggets about which scholars were previously unaware. As Tim Causer, the director of the project, says of the transcribers, "They make a genuine contribution to humanities research, as draft transcripts will act as a starting point for editors of [Bentham's] Collected Works volumes." And they will be acknowledged in those future books.

Bentham wrote in a script ranging from legible to almost impenetrable, and some letters cannot be read by laypeople: "He was writing until a few months before his death, and during the final years of his life his eyesight (and his handwriting) deteriorated very badly—this later material requires a specialist to try and decipher much of it," Causer points out. But with this project as with the others, a small group does the bulk of the work. "Most of the work has been done by a core of 25 volunteers," says Causer, "though 440 people have transcribed something." Other, similar programs include the "Transcribe the Renaissance," a one-day "transcribathon" held in conjunction with the University of Pennsylvania and the Folger Shakespeare Library[3] and the Smithsonian Digital Volunteers' Transcription Center.[4]

With the success of these initial crowdsourcing programs, the door can be opened to all sorts of handwriting that has been previously inaccessible. In that lies tremendous potential for future reclamation of the ephemeral past we do not want to lose. Libraries and institutions are developing tools and guidelines to enable individuals to digitize family documents; the National Archives has several guides. Some commercial options are available to have these documents transcribed as well, and scholars are working on additional transcription programs for anyone with a private manuscript collection. These would help me: Thirty years ago, before she died, my grandmother gave me handwritten notes about her life that she wrote in her final days. These fragments of her memoir are written on the backs of envelopes, on pages of drawing paper, on lined notebook paper, and other odd scraps of paper she had close by. They are hard to read. The paper is fragile. And carrying around these notes causes me anxiety—what if there is a fire? But a free, convenient way for me to scan those notes, have them transcribed and encoded, and then delivered back to me as an electronic file—as well as being searchable on the Web, should I choose to make them so—would be a boon to both my family and to the historical record. What would be a better way to preserve my familial, cultural, and historic connection to the past and pass it on to my child and future generations? There are enormous numbers of handwritten manuscripts that have never been available to the public, let alone transcribed; as these documents are digitized, translated, and made accessible, they will alter our understanding of history.

But as scrawled notes to lovers are put up on the Web, there is a growing nostalgia for handwriting, to see it as a more "authentic," "natural," and less mediated way to communicate. A similar longing, a century ago, led to the creation of calligraphy in the West.

Chapter 12

THE CONTINUAL REVIVAL OF
FANCY LETTERS

T HE AMERICAN GREETINGS world headquarters is
located on American Road in Cleveland, Ohio. A
large, anonymous glass building looming behind a curved,
wooded driveway, it houses gift shops, a cafeteria, and offices
for the two thousand employees who have survived the
downturn in the greeting card industry brought about by
e-cards and the economic recession.

Still employed by American Greetings are seven letterers
responsible for creating the look of the words that adorn
Mother's Day, graduation, and other celebratory cards. They
create new handwritten scripts—not fonts or typescripts—
that are later reproduced. The two most experienced ones,
who carry the title of senior letterer, have backgrounds in
calligraphy.

Calligraphic-trained letterers are a rare breed. Only

three major institutions have calligraphers on staff: American Greetings, Hallmark, and the White House. Although the world of full-time, professional letterers is tiny, the digital age is creating an upsurge of interest in the art of beautiful lettering.*

Calligraphy has long been an art in the Middle East and China, and it has always been linked to cultural and national values. Scholar Albertine Gaur calls calligraphy a "corporate logo" for cultures, "an expression of harmony as perceived by a particular civilization." The West has a weaker calligraphic tradition. It disappeared within generations after the invention of the printing press and was not revived until the latter half of the nineteenth century. Handwritten communication continued, of course, but the ceremonial, artistic practice of using specific scripts to commemorate and laud did not. As Gaur puts it, "The fact that more people wanted, and were able, to write brought about a leveling down of standards."[1]

William Morris and the Arts and Crafts Movement revived the work of medieval scribes. The movement was a clear response to the Industrial Revolution, with its machines and smog and printed letters. In addition to tapestries, wallpaper, and furniture using artisanal, preindustrial processes, Morris and his colleagues re-created the

---

* Calligraphers are trained in traditional Western scripts such as capitalis and copperplate. Letterers create new scripts.

writing materials, surfaces, habits, and scripts of the medieval monks.

Morris founded the Kelmscott Press in 1891 to publish letterpress books on handmade paper, and the Central School of Arts and Crafts was founded in 1896 to carry on his design philosophies. One of his friends, Edward Johnston, expanded on Morris's interest in medieval writing. "Since the traditions of the early scribes and printers and carvers have decayed, we have become so used to inferior forms and arrangements that we hardly realize how poor the bulk of modern lettering really is," Johnston wrote. He decided to study exactly how the monks wrote, and via manuscripts in the British Library (then the British Museum Library) he determined that monks held their pens differently to create the angles they did. He taught himself medieval writing techniques, such as how the nibs were cut and the parchment was ruled. Johnston began teaching these methods at the Central School and later at the Royal College of Art, single-handedly created a calligraphy movement in Britain, as well as helping other similar movements take root in America and Europe.

In 1906, Johnston published *Writing & Illuminating & Lettering*, an accessible, charming, and meticulous guide to how to write as the medieval monks did; chapters include how to cut pens, make upward and downward strokes, line pages, and master different hands. Johnston took the medieval revival so far as to recommend re-creating the working conditions of a scriptorium and writing only by natural light—never at night. Working through his book, a calligrapher-to-be first learned uncial and half-uncial, then Roman capitals, Roman small-letter (Roman rustic), and finally italics, or humanist script.

Although self-described revivers of the lost craft of the monks, Johnston's followers saw themselves as artists; unlike monks, they signed their names and chose handwriting over printing, an option unavailable to medieval scribes. Western calligraphy, a self-conscious celebration of fancy lettering in and of itself, is a wholly twentieth-century concept. So, too, is its popularity due to new technologies. Ironically, *Writing & Illuminating & Lettering*, reprinted dozens of times and still in use today, led to the revival of handwritten manuscripts.[2]

Eight years after Johnston's book was published, the trend was clear:

In recent years England has seen a notable revival of Calligraphy, that is to say of beautiful and formal handwriting. This revival has already had echoes on the continent and in America and bids fair eventually not only to lead to the wide production of highly finished manuscripts for those who can afford them, but also to influence for good, through school-teachers and improved copybooks in many countries, the types of handwriting and lettering now in vogue.[3]

The Society of Scribes & Illuminators was the first calligraphic association, founded in 1921 in London. This informal society called itself, as would others, a guild, in a nod to the medieval roots of their art. Guilds exhibited work and studied how to write on skins, prepare ink, and gild. Private classes and workshops were offered in England, Europe, and the United States, and the most serious students underwent informal apprenticeships with individual teachers.

In the United States, the calligraphic revival was fueled by this apprenticeship model. Ernst Frederick Detterer, an American, studied with Edward Johnston privately in London and returned to the United States to found a society in Chicago. Other individuals founded societies in other cities: New York (Society of Scribes); Portland, Oregon (Portland Society for Calligraphy); and Philadelphia (Philadelphia Calligraphers' Society). To this day, most trained calligraphers are members of these informal yet long-lasting guilds.

In the late 1960s and 1970s, calligraphy experienced a second revival for predictably similar reasons: hippies and other back-to-earthers, like those of the Arts and Crafts era, valued making things by hand in reaction to mass culture. The *Whole Earth Catalog*, that iconic book of the seventies, has a chapter dedicated to calligraphy, and a brisk business developed in calligraphy pens and instruction manuals and offering italics workshops.

During this resurgence both the senior letterers at American Greetings, Mike Gold and Martha Ericson, learned calligraphy. Gold, who grew up in California, was working with a sign painter who introduced him to lettering, the creation of letters in a recognizable design, as opposed to calligraphy, which is the re-creation of historic, formulaic scripts. Gold was initially more animated by lettering and was slower to appreciate the allure of the more rigid, imitative calligraphy: "I thought of it as just Old English; I didn't realize it was an art, too," he says, using the term "Old English" to refer to what I have been calling Gothic or blackletter. When Gold discovered copying scripts could be artistic and creative as well, he wanted to learn more scripts, but there were no classes to take. So he started corresponding with a well-known calligrapher in England, Roy Hampton. By writing letters to Hampton, Gold had an ad hoc, long-distance education.

The ranks of amateur calligraphers are growing, as "people want stuff made by hand again," as Gold puts it. He points to scrapbooking, journaling, and the rise of lettering books and artists such as John Stevens, author of *Scribe: Artist of the Written Word*, popular among graphic artists, as examples, as well as the lettered chalkboards increasingly popular in restaurants and higher-end grocery stores, and among brides who are requesting menus so ornate and precise they can take up to twenty hours to letter. Wedding invitation envelopes addressed in calligraphy are the bread and butter of amateur calligraphy. "Hire a calligrapher for your envelopes" is on many checklists in glossies like *Brides* magazine. Occasionally a calligrapher will be commissioned for a resolution or certificate. Diploma work dried up a while ago when degree-granting institutions shifted to Xerox.

Although few professional Western calligraphers reside in the United States, Muslims and Jews still hire trained experts to create copies of their religious texts. In both traditions, the calligrapher must be devout and undergo a long apprenticeship to learn the exacting laws prescribing how to write the holy texts of the Koran and the Torah, as well as other documents such as marriage announcements. In contrast to the West's boom-and-bust revival of calligraphy over the past century, Muslims and Jews have been so consistent about how their holy documents are written that their current practices remain precisely as they were a millennium or more ago. These traditional practices put into relief the modern reinterpretation that is calligraphy in the West.

Today, in response to the digital age, we are similarly "reviving"—or reinventing—handwriting as an art. On Etsy, a hugely popular website for artists and craftspeople that has the sheen of the preindustrial to it, you can buy computer-simulated handwriting: graphic designs that emulate print and cursive. You can also hire someone to handwrite invitations using "historic" or "old-fashioned–looking" letters.

The revived interest in artisanal handwriting as a hobby or art form brings us back to the question of Ellie's practical education and what to do in the American second and third grades. If we do not teach handwriting, will the cognitive abilities of children suffer? Does handwriting make us smarter?

Chapter 13

THE SCIENCE OF HANDWRITING

RESEARCH ON THE cognitive superiority of writing by hand over typing on a keyboard is all fairly recent, with scattered studies done to test a phalanx of different issues: literacy acquisition, speed of writing, test scores, and reading comprehension. There is no convincing empirical evidence that handwriting is cognitively superior to keyboarding, although some make that claim.

Scientific American published an article in 2013 titled "The Science of Handwriting" in which the only verifiable proof the author found is that people with brain lesions that make handwriting difficult also have difficulty recognizing letters. The rest of the "science" is pretty fuzzy, as the author, Brandon Keim, admits. Virginia Berninger, who calls the hand "the end organ of the language system," is cited in Keim's article. Berninger conducted a study that found students who could write the alphabet legibly and quickly had higher spelling and composition scores than those who could not, suggesting that good handwriting leads to better reading comprehension and writing ability. But she admits her findings are provisional and "need to be replicated." No comparable study has been done to analyze the scores of students who type quickly. Marieke Longcamp did a research study following established scientific protocols that showed people remembered letters better if they wrote them than if they typed them. However, Longcamp's study involved only a "few dozen" participants. Keim concludes his piece by doing his own experiment. Having written it longhand, "I can report, in this non-conclusive, N of 1 study, with no controls or standardized metrics or objective behavioral outcomes, that writing by hand felt good, even right."

Many people feel the same: Handwriting feels right. But that is due to our backgrounds and associations—almost all Americans alive today were taught to make letters with pencils in school. This has been true only for a few generations, though. Most humans over the long course of history never developed such associations, and thus have no childhood associations to make it "feel good" to write longhand.

There is conclusive science about reading acquisition: Reading does alter the brain. Once a person becomes literate and does not have to sound out letters, the brain is freed "from the effort of decoding—perhaps more so with an alphabet than with any other writing system—people are freed to think more, and to generate new thoughts."[1] Although humans were not "wired" for reading, once they invented it, neuronal pathways that were designed for vision and for other, related functions—like inferring that a footprint could mean danger—were used for reading. Writing further expanded the brain, according to Maryanne Wolf. "With each of the new writing systems, with their different increasingly sophisticated demands, the brain's circuitry rearranged itself, causing our repertoire of intellectual capacities to grow and change in great, wonderful leaps of thoughts."

But it is not a straight line of progress. Wolf, as noted in an earlier chapter, argues that ancient Egyptian writers may have evolved further than any other culture due to the complexity of their system. And those who learn Chinese develop different neuronal connections than do English writers. Even small differences matter, according to Wolf, whose research finds that brains process capital letters in a different neurological way than they do lowercase letters.

Each individual person's development follows somewhat this same evolutionary trend, just much, much more quickly. As Wolf puts it, "It took 2000 years to get from Sumer to Greek alphabet, but we expect our children to master it in 2000 days."[2] The linguist Steven Pinker uses another analogy: "Children are wired for sound, but print is an optional accessory that must be painstakingly bolted on."[3]

The key neurological function that we want to bolt into children's brains is cognitive automaticity, the ability to write without consciously being aware one is doing it. When the brain has automatized the slopes of letters or their place on a keyboard, it is freed from low-level demands. Ellie, the second grader discussed in the introduction, who finds both handwriting and typing hard, has not achieved cognitive automaticity in either. Once she does, her writing will improve, because two-thirds of composing is planning, regardless of the tool.[4] Psychology professor Ronald T. Kellogg, in *The Psychology of Writing*, states that "the tool choice makes no difference in determining how well a writer composes." Nor do people think better with a pen than on a keyboard: "This may be true for some writers at inspired moments or for those using a free-writing strategy, but as a general rule, it seems highly suspect. Planning and translating are generally highly effortful, controlled operations that proceed too slowly in general, not too rapidly, for the pen to match the pace."[5]

By fourth grade, Ellie will likely achieve cognitive automaticity whether she is using a pen or a keyboard. If she is typical, cursive will be her toughest challenge, and if she does not master cursive by fourth grade because of fine motor skills or other issues, she will continue to struggle with it—and never achieve cognitive automaticity in cursive—for the rest of her life.

If that happens, she will receive lower grades in school,

because students with poor handwriting receive worse scores on tests and essays. According to Steve Graham, Mary Emily Warner Professor in the Division of Leadership and Innovation in the Teachers College of Arizona State University, teachers grade neatly written essays higher than less legible papers, what he calls the "handwriting effect": "Teachers form judgments, positive or negative, about the literary merit of text based on its overall legibility," he finds. "When teachers rate multiple versions of the same paper differing only in terms of legibility, they assign higher grades to neatly written versions of the paper than the same versions with poorer penmanship." In another study done by the College Board, those who chose cursive over printing received higher scores.[6] Even further up the educational ladder, students can be unfairly assessed: Some college courses require blue-book exams, which must be handwritten.

There is no science that proves handwriting makes students smarter; further, typing clearly has a democratizing effect, removing unconscious bias against students with poor handwriting, and leveling the look of prose to allow expression of ideas, not the rendering of letters, to take center stage. Everyone is graded on the same curve. Odds are Ellie will be faster at typing than at writing by hand by the fourth grade, and she will rarely need to handwrite in school and work as she grows up. But she might choose to anyway.

OUR JOHN HANCOCKS

"JUST PUT YOUR John Hancock here," the car dealer or mortgage broker might say, and you know what he means. John Hancock's signature is something a vast majority of Americans can see in their minds' eye, those very large, very clear letters, complete with a flourish, those squiggles below the name. Hancock's round-hand script gained him robust posthumous fame. He became a synonym for what counts as legal proof of one's identity, one's personhood.

Signatures are one of the last lines of defense for pro-handwriting advocates. ("Imagine if our children cannot sign their names!") It is also a source of embarrassment and even shame for some: Without practice, handwriting atrophies. But the history of the signature as legal proof of identity is short. Being able to make one's mark—a cross or an X or a thumbprint—has been good enough for most of Western history, and since 2000, with the passage of the electronic signatures law, digitally clicking "I agree" has sufficed as a signature for huge swaths of bureaucracy. In terms of security, if one is concerned about authenticating identity, credit cards and SIM cards—newer forms of identity protection—are arguably more secure and sophisticated than signatures. But the signature retains cultural resonance, and John Hancock continues to be interchangeable with signing one's name. For this reason, National Handwriting Day is every January 23, on John Hancock's birthday.

National Handwriting Day is the brainchild of the Writing Instrument Manufacturers Association (WIMA) representing the $4.8 billion industry of pen, pencil, and marker manufacturers. A lobby located about a block away from the White House, WIMA was formed in 1943 "to bring together pen, marker and mechanical pencil industries." In 1994, in a moment of conglomeration, it merged with the Pencil Makers Association. They sponsor the national day, created in 1977, to celebrate handwriting's "purity." Their website contains information about industry standards, the history of the association, and "fun facts," such as "A typical pencil can draw a line 35 miles long or write about 45,000 words."

But the first words in the description of National Handwriting Day indicate a slight desperation: "Handwriting is an [*sic*] true art form and one of the few ways we can uniquely express ourselves." For the pen and pencil lobby to call handwriting a "lost art" indicates just how quickly the decline of handwriting has occurred—how different the sales pitch needs to be today than it would have been just twenty years ago: "Handwriting allows us to be artists and individuals during a time when we often use computers, faxes and e-mail to communicate. Fonts are the same no matter what computer you use or how you use it and they lack a personal touch. Handwriting can add intimacy to a letter and reveal details about the writer's personality."

This charming yet flummoxing lobby reminds us that handwriting is a business, since some of the outcry over the "lost art" is coming from those with a financial stake in keeping us writing thank-you notes on gift cards or teaching our students D'Nealian, the easier, stripped-down script invented in the 1970s by Donald Thurber and commonly taught in American schools today. Zaner-Bloser, the large and very profitable publisher of penmanship curricula, sponsors research studies and conferences often cited in press accounts of the importance of teaching penmanship; that the research was funded by a company invested in keeping us learning cursive is not readily apparent.

You know a technology has officially become antiquated when it becomes, like vinyl records, mainly emblematic, a form of hipster cool, and evidence shows that handwriting, particularly cursive, has made this transition: A store called Cursive New York opened up in Grand Central Terminal in Manhattan in 2009. Among twentysomethings, getting literary tattoos—quotes from famous novels or lines of poetry—is popular, and many ask their tattoo artists to ink the quotes in cursive. One woman featured at Contrariwise, a website devoted to literary tattoos, has a Shakespeare quote: "Sleep thou, and I will winde thee in my army," done in a careful italic script. Book publishers must find that handwriting sells, because book jacket designs, like the one on this book, are increasingly being printed in fonts that emulate script. Several programs allow one to create an entire font based on your handwriting.

Some consumer electronics are encouraging a return to handwriting. Electronic tablets are now being released with styluses, and Samsung Galaxy included a stylus with its smartphone to allow people to write notes directly on the screen. In an ad for Galaxy, teenage girls revise each other's poems in class by writing in clichéd teen-girl script: big, rounded letters with hearts to dot *i*'s. "Because life needs more than texts, smiley-faces and xoxo's," the text on the screen proclaims. Then a child is shown writing "Wish you were here!" over a picture on the screen, and we are told that this is "a pen so smart it [can make] something no one else can."

Handwriting remains the dominant writing technology in prison. Although I received thousands of responses to my previous writing on this topic, I have received only three handwritten responses, all of which were sent from inmates, and came in envelopes stamped "INMATE MAIL" across the front. "Dear Professor Trubek," begins one, the letters uniform and graceful. "Although I am incarcerated in a state prison in Pennsylvania I hold both undergraduate and graduate degrees in the biological sciences. I have vivid memories of ink wells and the accompanying pens in my elementary school desks—I can also remember the cursive script of the alphabet, both capital and small letters, above the blackboard." He writes how he was praised for his handwriting and received an A in eighth-grade penmanship in West Scranton Junior/ Senior High School in Scranton, Pennsylvania.

The second letter is also written on lined notebook paper, and the writer has extraordinarily stylized script, the cross on the *t* always at a perfect 45-degree angle, the loop on the *d*'s huge and regular. It is so pretty, it resists reading: One wants to simply admire the patterns. So I was surprised to read his words: "The keyboard has made the usefulness or should I say rendered the usefulness of handwriting these days, partially obsolete. In fact, I'd go on to say, that outside of senior citizens and shut-ins and lest I forget, we prisoners, handwriting, is something no longer practical nor utilized." Despite not having access to keyboards—and he is part of a growing, not decreasing, population who cannot access keyboards—he can accept handwriting becoming obsolete.

But many eighteen-year-olds resist any proposed curricular changes to reduce handwriting instruction. In a course I taught at Oberlin College, "Technologies of Writing: From Plato to the Digital Age," every student balked at the idea that handwriting might not be taught to elementary school students. They were quick to offer examples of why handwriting is important. "If you were on a desert island, you would not be able to spell 'SOS.'" "The things I write in my notebook are more permanent than what I write on my computer." "What would we do if the lights go out?" I quickly found faults in their logic, and eventually most conceded that a primarily emotional attachment to handwriting made them argue for its continued place in the American school system: They were raised in a culture that connected handwriting to individual expression and personality, and it forms some of their earliest memories of schooling.

My son, Simon, would have been thrilled if handwriting had been left out of his elementary school education. When he was in second grade, in 2006, he had to stay in for recess almost every day because he could not properly form his letters. I was called in for "interventions" and warned that he would fail the fourth-grade Ohio Proficiency Test if scanners could not read his test answers.

For Simon, homework was terrifying, as it was dominated by penmanship exercises. He would stare at a blank page for an hour. Then he would write one word and then stop, write a few letters and then stop. Soon, he began to fear taking up a pencil at all, and we had nightly battles over his language arts worksheets. He began to worry about not having anything to say, not knowing how to say it, or he would come up with ideas that he would not write down because they would take too long, and thus he would write nothing. Perennially being told his handwriting was bad transmuted in his mind into proof that he was a bad writer—a poor student incapable of expressing ideas. He simply hated the physical process of writing. And since handwriting dominated his education in grades one, two, and three, he hated school, too.

I feel for any student assessed on his intelligence based on the quality of his penmanship. Most of my family is penmanship challenged, being a strong line of left-handers, and like many lefties I have always had poor handwriting. I don't have many vivid memories of my earliest years, but I do have a very distinct recollection of receiving an "NI," "Needs improvement," on my second-grade report card. I know well what it is like to be taught by people who, as one second-grade teacher told me, believe that "it makes people seem more intelligent if they can write clearly."

In 2010, the Common Core State Standards Initiative advised all school districts in the United States on what they should teach at each grade level. Strikingly, the new standards pay scant attention to handwriting. In fact, the only time handwriting appears is in kindergarten and first grade, when students are "expected to be able to write legibly." Instead, the Common Core State Standards Initiative focuses more heavily on typing standards: by the end of fourth grade, students should "demonstrate sufficient command of keyboarding skills to type a minimum of one page in a single sitting."[1] Many school districts were taken aback by the lack of printing and cursive standards, and some rejected them. Since states are allowed to expand on the standards, some have put handwriting back in. In a recent example, New Hampshire lobbied that cursive should be put back into the curriculum using conservative rhetoric, arguing cursive is as important as reciting the Pledge of Allegiance each day. A Catholic school advertises for students by describing its advantages over public schools: a dress code, teaching of moral values, and cursive writing.[2]

Our concerns over handwriting tell us as much about us as they do about technology. We are all, like Ellie, living through a transitional moment. Although we may disagree on the merits and demerits of cursive instruction, few would argue that we are writing less than we were a generation ago. If anything, we are in a golden age of writing: Most Americans write hundreds if not thousands more words a day than they did ten or twenty years ago.

We have supplanted much talking and phone calling with texting, e-mailing, and social media. One of the most surprising aspects of the digital revolution, in fact, is how very text based it has been. As we keep writing more on different surfaces, we create new methods of making letters: We press our fingers onto glass, we swipe across touch screens, and we talk to Siri, dictating our words to a digital scribe, just as Socrates, Caesar, the popes, royals, and novelists of the past did. The pace of change (with the exception of our stubborn commitment to the QWERTY keyboard) has been so rapid, it is easy to forget how quickly and sweepingly we have changed.

If the history recounted here repeats itself, there will be less heterogeneity soon; keyboarding—perhaps done by swiping instead of pressing—will become ubiquitous in American elementary classrooms, and we will develop new cultural, emotional, and individual associations with the rhythm and look and feel of pressing letters, ones that we may then impart to our children when they learn to write. Meanwhile, handwriting will shift in meaning yet again. Preserving handwriting's artistic aspects, be it through calligraphy or mastering comic-book lettering, is worthy. In schools, we might transition to teaching handwriting in art class or specifically as a fine motor skill, and encourage calligraphers as we do letterpress printers and stained glass window makers. These arts have a life beyond nostalgia.

Not for a long time will handwriting cease to be taught at all—for us to have the interview with the "last handwriter" as we do today with the last living speakers of some languages. By 1600 B.C.E. all Sumerian speakers had died, but people did not stop writing Sumerian for another thousand years, until 600 B.C.E. Even the revolutionary Greeks spent four hundred years doing little with writing, preferring their oral culture. The shift away from handwriting will bring about losses. But those losses will also give rise to changes—in accessibility, in democratization, in advantages unimaginable to us now—that should be celebrated.

ACKNOWLEDGMENTS

I have the good fortune of living in a community that supports writing: a Creative Workforce Fellowship, granted by Cuyahoga Arts and Culture, enabled the writing of this book: I thank, profusely, the voters of Cuyahoga County.

I am indebted to those who offered feedback along the way: Michael Jauchen, Denise Grollmus, Mark Athitakis, Martha Bayne, Gabriel Brownstein, Karen Long, and Kristen Ohlson, as well as Michael Jauchen and Sarah Rettger. Special thanks go to Meredith Hindley and Jennifer Howard for their unflagging support both intellectual and emotional. I am grateful to those who took the time to help me understand their work on cuneiform, calligraphy, paleography, forensic examining, stylometrics, and other topics along the way, and this book was also improved by Oberlin College students in various iterations of my course, Technologies of Writing: From Plato to the Digital Age, who had to handwrite an essay for one assignment, causing no shortage of frustration or laughter. The book was also improved by the baristas at Phoenix Coffee on Lee Road in Cleveland Heights, where I spent countless hours drafting chapters on my laptop.

To my editor, George Gibson, whose (handwritten) edits and support through this process taught me how to be a better writer, and my agent, Andrew Blauner, whose enthusiasm and responsiveness kept me going: thank you. And, finally, of course, to my son, Simon, whose struggles with penmanship in elementary school gave me the idea for this book. He now types eighty words per minute.

NOTES

Chapter One

1 I have used the following books for my research on cunei-
form: Jean-Jacques Glassner, *The Invention of Cuneiform*
(Baltimore: Johns Hopkins University Press, 2003); Steven
Roger Fischer, *The History of Writing* (London: Reaktion
Books, 2001); C. F. B. Walker, *Reading the Past: Cuneiform*
(London: British Museum Press, 1987); Barry B. Powell,
Writing: Theory and History of the Technology of Civilization
(Oxford: Wiley-Blackwell, 2012); Leila Avrin, *Scripts, Scribes
and Books: The Book Arts from Antiquity to the Renaissance* (New
York: American Library Association, 1991); James Gleick, *The
Information: A History, a Theory, a Flood* (New York: Pantheon,
2011); and Nicholas Ostler, *Empires of the Word: A Language
History of the World* (New York: HarperCollins, 2005). Good
summaries of proto-writing, and debates on what counts as
writing and what does not, can be found in Denise Schmandt-
Besserat's well-regarded but contested theory in *How Writing
Came About* (Austin: University of Texas Press, 2010); in
Powell, *Writing*; and in Gleick, *The Information*.

Chapter Two

1 For further reading on ancient Egyptian writing, see Powell, *Writing*, and Fischer.

2 Both quotes from J. T. Hooker, *Reading the Past: Ancient Writing from Cuneiform to the Alphabet* (London: British Museum Press, 1990), 101.

3 Powell, 11.

4 Ibid., 15.

5 Ibid., 15.

Chapter Three

1 Phaedrus by Plato. Translated by Benjamin Jewett, http://classics.mit.edu/Plato/phaedrus.1b.txt.

2 Ibid.

3 For a discussion of speech versus writing, see Roland Barthes, "From Speech to Writing," in Roland Barthes, *The Grain of the Voice: Interviews 1962–1980*, translated by Linda Coverdale (New York: Hill and Wang, 1985), 3–8.

4 Walter Ong, "Some Psychodynamics of Orality," in *Perspectives on Literacy*, edited by Eugene R. Kintgen, Barry M. Kroll, and Mike Rose (Carbondale and Edwardsville: Southern Illinois University Press, 1988), 30.

5 King James Bible.

6 Avrin, 145.

7 Stephanie Pappas, "Pompeii 'Wall Posts' Reveal Ancient Social Networks," Live Science, January 10, 2013, http://www.livescience.com/26164-pompeii-wall-graffiti-social-networks.html.

8 Avrim, 111.

9 http://news.discovery.com/history/archaeology/curse-ancient-roman-lead-scroll-120821.htm.

10 http://news.discovery.com/history/archaeology/curse-ancient-roman-lead-scroll-120821.htm.

11 Martial, Epigrams 4.89, *Martial Epigrams: Volume 1*, translated by D. R. Shackleton Bailey, (Cambridge, MA: Harvard University Press), 1993.

CHAPTER FOUR

1 Many Greek and Roman works were not copied in the West during the medieval era, given their non-Christian content, but they were preserved by Byzantines and Muslims in the Near East.

2 As quoted in Alberto Manguel, *The History of Reading* (New York: Penguin, 1996), 45.

3 Theophilus, *De diversis artibus* (The Various Arts), edited by C. R. Dodwell (Oxford, UK: Oxford University Press, 1987).

4 As quoted in Manguel, 50.

5 Saint Augustine, "Concerning the Trinity," xv, 10:19, in *Basic Writings of Saint Augustine*, edited by Whitney J. Oates (New York: Random House, 1948).

6 Mary Carruthers, *Rhetoric Beyond Words: Delight and Persuasion in the Arts of the Middle Ages.* (Cambridge, UK: Cambridge University Press, 2010), 132.

7 Quoted in Colin Dickey, "Living In the Margins," Lapham's Quarterly, http://www.laphamsquarterly.org/roundtable/living-margins.

8 Christopher de Hamel, *Medieval Craftsmen: Scribes and Illuminators* (Toronto: University of Toronto Press, 1992), 7.

9 Albertine Gaur, *A History of Calligraphy* (New York: Cross River Press, 1994), 77.

10 C. R. Dodwell, *The Pictorial Arts of the West, 800–1200*, Vol. 7 (New Haven, CT: Yale University Press, 1995), 246.

CHAPTER FIVE

1 Juan-Jose Marcos, "Fonts for Latin Paleography," June 2014, http://guindo.pntic.mec.es/jmago042/LATIN_PALEOGRAPHY.pdf.

2 This summary of medieval scripts, particularly post–Roman rustic, is necessarily schematic and incomplete, as there were a dizzying number of hands used. Nor were book hands, what I discuss here, the only kind of writing: There were also innumerable chancery hands, or scripts used for writing anything that was not a manuscript, developed during this 1,500-year period. The texts I used for this chapter, which include in-depth discussions of medieval scripts, include Avrin, *Scripts, Scribes and Books*; De Hamel, *Scribes and Illuminators*; Michelle P. Brown, *The British Library Guide to Writing and Scripts: History and Techniques* (Toronto: University of Toronto Press, 1998); Bernhard Bischoff, *Latin Palaeography: Antiquity and the Middle Ages*, translated by Dáibhi ó Cróinín and David Ganz (Cambridge, UK: Cambridge University Press, 1990); Stanley Morison, *Politics and Script: Aspects of Authority and Freedom in the Development of Graeco-Latin Script from the Sixth-Century BC* (Oxford, UK: Oxford University Press, 2000); and Albertine Gaur, *A History of Calligraphy* (New York: Cross River, 1994).

3 Jill Kraye, *Cambridge Companion to Renaissance Humanism* (Cambridge, UK: Cambridge University Press, 1996), page 60.

4 Bracciolini, a scribe who rose in ranks to become papal secretary and is discussed later in this chapter, is the subject of Stephen Greenblatt's *The Swerve: How the World Became Modern* (New York: W. W. Norton, 2011).

5 Morison, *Politics and Script*, page 326–7.

CHAPTER SIX

1   Johannes Trithemius, *In Praise of Scribes: De laude scriptorum* (Vancouver, BC: Alcuin Society, 1977).

2   As quoted in Clay Shirky, *Cognitive Surplus: How Technology Makes Consumers into Collaborators* (New York: Penguin, 2011).

3   As quoted in *Syon Abbey and Its Books: Reading, Writing and Religion, c. 1400–1700,* edited by E. A. Jones and Alexandra Walsham (Suffolk, Martlesham, UK: Boydell & Brewer, 2010), 110.

4   As quoted in A.S. Osley, *Scribes and Sources: Handbook of the Chancery Hand in the 16th Century* (Boston: D.R. Godine, 1980), 17.

5   *The Complete Work of Charles Dickens: The Pickwick Papers, Vol. 11.* (New York: Cosimo Classics, 2009), 435.

6   Martin Billingsley, *The Pens Excellencie* (1618).

7   Literacy rates are very hard to confirm, and scholars debate which methods should be used and how to estimate rates. For the best discussion of this debate for Colonial literacy as well as reading and writing instruction in eighteenth-century America, see E. Jennifer Monaghan, *Learning to Read and Writing in Colonial America* (Amherst: University of Massachusetts Press, 2005).

8   Tamara Plakins Thornton, *Handwriting in America: A Cultural History* (New Haven: Yale University Press, 1996), 8.

9   Ibid., 9.

10 Monaghan, 281.

11 David McCollough, *John Adams* (New York: Simon & Schuster, 2001).

12 Thomas De Quincey, *Confessions of an Opium Eater* (New York: Penguin, 2003), 80.

Chapter Seven

1 See Thornton for a fuller discussion of Spencer and his legacy.
2 H. C. Spencer and Platt Rogers Spencer, *Spencerian Key to Practical Penmanship: Prepared for the "Spencerian Authors"* (Ithaca, NY: Cornell University Press, 2009).
3 As quoted in Thornton, 49.
4 *Theory of the Spencerian System of Practical Penmanship in Nine Easy Lessons*. Originally published in 1874; reprinted by Mott Media.
5 Kitty Burns Florey, *Script and Scribble: The Rise and Fall of Handwriting* (New York: Melville House, 2008), 71.
6 Thornton, 66.
7 *Cincinnati Public Schools: Eighty-fifth Annual Report* (Cincinnati, 1915), 71.
8 The Palmer Method of Business Writing, http://palmer-method.com.
9 Ibid.
10 Ibid.
11 Ibid.
12 Ibid.
13 Ibid.
14 Thornton, 158.
15 Thornton, 152.
16 Angel Kwokel-Folland, *Engendering Business: Men and Women in the Corporate Office, 1870–1930* (Baltimore: Johns Hopkins University Press, 1994), 30.

Chapter Eight

1 Bruce Bliven Jr. *The Wonderful Writing Machine* (New York: Random House, 1954), 42.
2 Ibid.

3   Mark Twain, "First Writing Machine," in *The $30,000 Bequest and Other Stories* (New York: Oxford, 1996).

4   Ibid.

5   Ibid.

6   Mark Seltzer, *Henry James and the Art of Power* (Ithaca: Cornell University Press, 1984), 202.

7   Pamela Thurschwell, "Henry James and Theodora Bosanquet: on the typewriter, *In the Cage* and the Ouija Board," in *Textual Practice* 13, no. 1 (1999), 6.

8   Seltzer, 201.

9   Thruschwell et al., 13.

10 Seltzer, 201.

11 Bliven, 102.

12 Ibid., 134.

13 Ibid., 139.

14 Thornton, 178.

15 "Of Lead Pencils," *New York Times*, August 22, 1938, page 12.

16 Bliven, 127.

17 Ibid., 128.

CHAPTER NINE

1   George Boys-Stones, Jas Elsner, Antonella Ghersetti, Robert Hoyland, Ian Repath, *Seeing the Face, Seeing the Soul: Polemon's Physiognomy from Classical Antiquity to Medieval Islam* (Oxford: Oxford University Press, 2007), 591.

2   Joe Nickell, *Detecting Forgery: Forensic Investigation of Documents* (Lexington: University of Kentucky Press, 2005), 17.

3   Ibid., 18.

4   Camillo Baldi, *A Method to Recognize the Nature and Quality of a Writer from His Letters* (1662), translated by Robert Backman in *Camillo Baldi, His Life and Works* (Greenfield, MA: Handwriting Analysis Research Library, 1994), 36.

5   As quoted in Thornton, 77.

6   Ibid., 79.

7   Ibid., 87.

8   Ibid., 88.

9   Isaac D'Israeli, *Curiosities of Literature* (London, 1838). Accessed via Google Books.

10 Ibid.

11 For more on the history of graphology, see Joe Nickell, "A Brief History of Graphology," in *The Write Stuff: Evaluations of Graphology, the Study of Handwriting Analysis*, edited by Barry Beyerstein and Dale F. Beyerstein (Amherst, NY: Prometheus, 1992).

12 Shaike Landau, "Michon, and the Birth of Scientific Graphology," http://www.britishgraphology.org/wp-content/ uploads/2012/02/MichonAndTheBirthOfScientificGraphology .pdf.

13 Ibid.

14 Ibid.

15 See Nickell, 25–26.

16 As quoted in Thornton, 94.

17 Arthur Storey *A Manual of Graphology or the Study of Handwriting* (London: William Rider & Son, 1922), 18.

18 Ibid., 10.

19 European Code of Dentology, http://adeg-europe.eu/wp- content/uploads/2015/09/European-Code-of-Deontology .pdf.

20 "A French Love Affair . . . with Graphology," BBC News Magazine, April 29, 2013, http://www.bbc.com/news/ magazine-22198554.

21 Ibid.

22 Andrea McNichol with Jeffrey A. Nelson, *Handwriting Analysis: Putting It to Work for You* (New York: McGraw-Hill, 1994).

Chapter Ten

1   Jennifer L. Mnookin, "Scripting Expertise: The History of Handwriting Identification Evidence and the Judicial Construction of Reliability," *Virginia Law Review* 87, no. 8, Symposium: New Perspectives on Evidence (Dec. 2001), 1723–1845. 1738.

2   Ibid., 1742.

3   Ibid., 1743.

4   Darren Wershler-Henry, *Iron Whim: A Fragmented History of the Typewriter* (Ithaca, NY: Cornell University Press, 2007), 178.

5   Ibid., 179.

6   Mnookin, 1765.

7   My discussion of the British and American legal history of handwriting as evidence relies on Jennifer Mnookin's "Scripting Evidence."

8   Mnookin, 1766.

9   As quoted in Mnookin, 1776.

10   Ibid., 1777.

11   Ibid., 1784.

12   Ibid., 1811.

13   Ibid., 1812.

14   Ibid., 1813.

15   For further reading on stylometrics, see Jeffrey Kahan, "'I Tell You What Mine Author Says': A Brief History of Stylometrics," *ELH* 82, no. 3 (Fall 2015), 815–44.

Chapter Eleven

1   Sections of this chapter were previously published in the *Atlantic*.

2   http://menus.nypl.org/about.

3 http://sceti.library.upenn.edu/Transcribathon/.

4 https://transcription.si.edu.

Chapter Twelve

1 Gaur, 19.

2 Edward Johnston, *Writing & Illuminating & Lettering* (London: Pitman, 1965).

3 Sidney Cockerell (1945), "Tributes to Edward Johnston" in *Lessons in Formal Writing*, edited by H. Child and J. Howes (London: Lund Humphries, 1986), 21–30.

Chapter Thirteen

1 Maryanne Wolf, *Proust and the Squid: The Story and Science of the Reading Brain* (New York: Harper, 2008), 13.

2 Wolf, 18–19.

3 As quoted in Wolf, 18.

4 J. D. Gould, "Experiments on Composing Letters: Some Facts, Some Myths, and Some Observations." In L. W. Gregg & E. R. Steinberg (Eds.), *Cognitive Processes in Writing* (pp. 97–128). Hillsdale, NJ: Erlbaum.

5 Ron Kellogg, *The Psychology of Writing* (Oxford: Oxford University Press, 1999).

6 https://research.collegeboard.org/sites/default/files/publications/ 2012/7/researchnote-2007-32-sat-writing-research-psychometrics .pdf.

Conclusion

1 Common Core English Language Arts Standards, Writing, Grade 4, http://www.corestandards.org/ELA-Literacy/W/4/.

2 Advertisement for Holy Cross, South Portland, Maine.

INDEX

A NOTE ON THE AUTHOR

ANNE TRUBEK IS the founder and director of Belt Publishing. She has published articles in the *New York Times*, the *Atlantic*, *Wired*, and many other publications. She is the author of *A Skeptic's Guide to Writers' Houses* and lives in Cleveland, Ohio.